HOW TO QUIT GOLF

HOW TO QUIT GOLF

A 12-STEP
PROGRAM

CRAIG BRASS

DUTTON

DUTTON
Published by the Penguin Group
Penguin Putnam Inc., 375 Hudson Street,
New York, New York 10014, U.S.A.
Penguin Books Ltd, 80 Strand, London WC2R 0RL, England
Penguin Books Australia Ltd, Ringwood, Victoria, Australia
Penguin Books Canada Ltd, 10 Alcorn Avenue,
Toronto, Ontario, Canada M4V 3B2
Penguin Books (N.Z.) Ltd, 182–190 Wairau Road, Auckland 10,
New Zealand

Penguin Books Ltd, Registered Offices: Harmondsworth,
Middlesex, England

First published by Dutton, a member of Penguin Putnam Inc.

First Printing, November, 2001
3   5   7   9   10   8   6   4   2

 REGISTERED TRADEMARK—MARCA REGISTRADA

Hostess is a registered trademark of Interstate Bakeries Corporation.

LIBRARY OF CONGRESS CATALOGING-IN-PUBLICATION DATA

Brass, Craig.
How to quit golf : a 12-step program / Craig Brass.
p.   cm.
ISBN 0-525-94629-2 (alk. paper)
1. Golf—Humor. I. Title.
GV967.B75 2001
796.352—dc21   2001033379

Printed in the United States of America
Set in Souvenir Light
Designed by Eve L. Kirch

To Beverly and Cameron,
who don't deserve to have a golfer
as a husband and a father

Foreword

by Jeff Daniels

As an actor, I used to play a lot of golf. I'd play between movies, on location, in celebrity tournaments, corporate outings, with my friends, my kids, and strangers. It didn't matter. Need a fourth? I was there. No cart? I'll walk. Rain or shine. I loved the game and everything about it. For me, golf was a Beach Boys song come to life—nothing but fun, fun, fun.

Then a funny thing happened. I shot a 79.

Now, as far as I'm concerned, breaking 80 is like turning 35; your life is suddenly nothing but a series of down-hill putts. Once you've broken that eighteen-hole benchmark you have jumped off the cliff and entered the free fall down into the Black Hole known as "Par or Death."

You work harder. You put in more time. More rounds. More instruction. Custom-fit your clubs. Analyze your game with a glove, without a glove. Keep season-long tallies of all your greens in regulation, drives in the fairway, number of putts, sand saves, scores in your blue shirt, your red shirt, your green shirt until one day, all of a sudden, for no reason, you will not be able to hit the ball. And when I say not hit the ball, I mean not hit the ball.

Sure, there will be occasional contact, but the swing, the "I am a Man of the 70s and I Don't Mean the Decade" swing you have perfected, studied, researched, carved from stone, sculpted into something seemingly everlasting, will be gone.

Like an aging athlete possessed, you will go back to your second home, the Driving Range, and hit bucket after bucket after bucket. Beating balls deep into the night in a quest to find that thing that is no longer there. Your head pro will saunter past, make a couple of suggestions and only make it worse. Your friends, trying to be helpful, will make comments, and confusion will reign.

Your monthly *Golf Digest* will read like Latin. You will talk to your clubs and they will talk back in a tone you haven't heard before. Years will pass—yes, years—until finally, one early spring day, after taking the winter off because of a miserable performance in last year's Club Championship in which you finished not only out of the money, but out of the money in the Fourth Flight, you will walk out to your garage to take your clubs out of storage and you will only get as far as the door.

You will stop and stare at your $500 custom-made golf bag, your $400 plutonium driver, your state-of-the-art irons, your flood-tested drip-dry golf shoes, and you will realize a simple, basic truth: You cannot lose something you never had. Here's another truth: In a world where nothing is what it seems, who needs that kind of crap during their leisure time?

Not too long ago, Craig Brass and I were, as we often did, putting up with this kind of crap during a casual round. When we both turned a routine par into yet another pair of triple bogeys, he looked at me and said, "Why do we do this to ourselves?" For the life of me I couldn't answer him, and instead of driving on to the next tee we just sat there, staring out blankly, as if we were living the end of a meaningless movie.

They say there are only two ways to quit the game of golf: a frontal lobotomy or this book. I recommend the book; it's cheaper and won't leave a scar. So like a good caddy, let Craig show you the way out of the woods. Take it from me, it might just be the best thing you've done since . . . well, since you broke 80.

My sole ambition in golf is to get good enough to give it up. —David Feherty

The most exquisitely satisfying act in the world of golf is that of throwing a club.

—Henry Longhurst

Your financial cost can best be figured when you realize that if you were to devote the same time and energy to business instead of golf, you would be a millionaire in approximately six weeks.

—Buddy Hackett

It took me seventeen years to get three thousand hits in baseball. I did it in one afternoon on the golf course. —Hank Aaron

I guess there is nothing that will get your mind off everything like golf. I have never been depressed enough to take up the game, but they say you get so sore at yourself you forget to hate your enemies. —Will Rogers

Always throw clubs ahead of you. That way you don't have to waste energy going back to pick them up. —Tommy Bolt

Take three weeks off and then quit the game.
—Sam Snead, purportedly to a struggling student

You Have a Problem

Before we get started, we must make something crystal clear. Quitting golf isn't going to be easy. You didn't become this big of a mess overnight, what with slicing, hooking, topping, shanking, chunking, three-putting, four-putting, and yipping all over the place. We can't just snap our fingers and make this go away. That's why we've developed the 12-step program *How to Quit Golf*.

Twelve-step programs are proven world-beaters. When it comes to knocking down the powers of addiction there is nothing better. And if you don't think golf is an addiction, why do you still subject yourself to slicing, hooking, topping, shanking, chunking, three-putting, four-putting, and yipping all over the place?

The only way to eradicate this problem, to clean up this mess if you will, is through the teachings and guidance of this book. If this program is going to work, however, you're going to need to understand and accept two basic fundamentals—what golf is, and what golf is not.

To begin with, golf is not a mystical game. It was not

invented by magical, spiritual beings as an exercise to heighten awareness or offer meaning to life. It is not a metaphor for anything, other than perhaps what lengths man will go to work himself into a boiled frenzy over the most insignificant issue.

Golf is not a subset of some highly enlightened, Zen-based Eastern religion that if mastered will bring you closer to total consciousness. It doesn't offer a glimpse inside your, or anyone else's, soul.

Golf cannot provide you with sanctity, cannot tighten bonds between men, and cannot deliver you to a place you couldn't get to on your own. If you're asking this of golf, you may as well be asking this of a dead cat.

What golf is, on the other hand, is a nasty, vicious game, played mainly by educated people who quite frankly should know better than to keep playing this sport.

You may feel this is a strong indictment to throw down against the game, but consider this. Through the years you've more than likely asked yourself the following questions: Why do I continue to wildly hook or slice the ball? Why do I always hit the ball into the same pond? Why do I suck so bad I want to throw myself into traffic? Why don't I just quit this stupid game? We assume that these questions have proven unanswerable.

Everyone who has ever sliced a drive or missed a gimme putt has at one time or another declared that they were going to quit the game, and who can blame them? Playing golf is like trying to go up a down escalator while bouncing on a pogo stick. Sure, you may know what you're trying to do. But the execution is brutally flawed, and you more often than not fail to achieve the desired results.

A golf course has boundaries, a golf ball doesn't. They go absolutely everywhere. They go in rough, sand and water. They shatter windows, shatter bones, and shatter dreams. Even tour professionals at times hit balls everywhere but where they want. Ever suffer along while watching Greg Norman try to win at Augusta?

It can be pointed out that Norman, who has suffered more heartbreaking setbacks on the golf course than anyone, hasn't quit. He keeps having at it, and if he's still out there giving it his best shot, why shouldn't everyone else keep trying?

He hasn't quit for the same reason you haven't been able to quit, which is the same reason no one can quit—as hard as the game is, it's even harder to quit.

The issue at hand isn't the desire to quit, but the ability to quit. First of all, nobody needs to play golf. Secondly, everybody who plays golf knows they don't need to play golf. The problem is nobody knows how to quit. Golf has a beginning, a middle, but no end. The game has no exit strategy.

Walk through any major bookstore in the country and there are thousands of books on golf. *How to Play Golf; How to Play Golf Better; How to Play Really Better Golf; Golf for Kids; Golf for Women; Golf for Pets; Where to Play Golf; Where Not to Play Golf; The Mental Game of Golf; The Physical Game of Golf; The Existential Game of Golf; How to Make Chicken Soup from Golf Balls, Tees and Divots;* and *I'm OK, You're OK, but the Golfer in the Corner Is Screwed Up Beyond Hope.*

Yet, with all that has been written on how to start golfing and keep golfing, nothing has been written on how to stop golfing. The explanation for this is clear. The elements working to keep golfers in a static level of dependency make the marketing staffs of the tobacco industry look like the golf writers playing Augusta National from the back tees on the Monday after the Masters.

Many golfers feel weak and helpless because they can't muster the strength to walk away from the game by themselves. This is understandable. Golfers are weak and helpless, but it's not entirely their fault. Golf teases, lures, and seduces us to try again, to give it another shot. By offering a drive or two down the middle, a great recovery shot, a birdie on the hardest hole, or anything at all of which golfers can boast, golf is in essence passing out free drug samples on the playground.

Golf entices you to come back. As if saying, "You're almost there, just a little more work and you'll get it. Any day now you'll have the game figured out, and when you do you'll be envy of all." But it's not going to happen. You're never going to get any better at this game. No one is ever going to get any better at this game.

Technological advances in golf have paralleled those in fields such as biotechnology, telecommunications, and personal computers. New genetic-based drugs are being developed every day. The PC on your desktop has more power than what was used to run the Apollo space missions. Anybody can reach anyone virtually anywhere in the world with the touch of a button.

Drivers are loaded with springlike faces that rocket balls down the straight and narrow. Golf balls have multiple layers of various materials and dimensions, and it's almost to the point where you can yell at them and they'll listen. But even with all of this, no one is getting any better at golf. The average handicap today is the same as it was twenty years ago.

In any other commercial venture there would be an outcry for an investigation to unearth the causes of this inertia. Yet no one has peered behind golf's satin curtain to expose the evils that lurk. Golf just stands there, with the precocious smirk of a six-year-old boy that claims he has no idea of who put the cat's tail in the electric outlet, while still grasping a handful of singed fur behind his back.

The fact is that golf is as innocent as O.J., but at least it's not as smug. Golf isn't pretending to be looking for the real reason you can't quit; it just doesn't feel like telling you. But we will: You can't give up the game because golf is the most addictive substance in all of nature. Golf is the one-armed bandit of the sporting world, the crack cocaine of the recreation industry.

Now, for the first time, we have outlined the addictive nature of the game, along with all of the underpinnings that make golf the asylum of lunatics, and the refuge of lost souls.

Many will question if golf is really a crisis that we should concern ourselves with. In the year 2000 the National Golf Foundation (NGF) estimated that there were 26.4 million golfers age twelve and over in the United States. Approximately six million of these golfers play more than twenty-one rounds per year. These people are characterized as avid golfers. Avid is such a benign term for people who are teetering on the brink of insanity.

If someone spends more than twenty-one afternoons a year throwing back shots of Stoli, do we call that person an avid drinker? Of course not, we call him a former member of the Soviet Politburo. If a person shoots heroin into his veins more than twenty-one times a year is he referred to as an avid intravenous drug user? Absolutely not, he's a junkie.

Labeling these golfers as avid softens the severity of the situation. Golfing, especially avid golfing, is an issue of national alarm, and needs to be taken as seriously as poverty, health care, gun control, and the impending collapse of the Medicaid and Medicare systems. Issues of this magnitude need important sounding names. We classify these six million people not as avid golfers, but as *problem golfers*.

This crisis isn't going away. Since 1986 the number of golfers in this country has increased 33 percent. If that pace continues, by the year 2013 there will be more than thirty-five million golfers in the United States, eight million of whom will be problem golfers. This screams epidemic. If golf were classified as a disease, as we believe it should be, Junior Leagues across the country would hold charity golf tournaments to raise money to fight it.

The NGF also estimates that the typical golfer is male, thirty-nine years old, and plays twenty rounds per year. This is also the age of the typical father with young children. At a time when this parent should be home doting over his children, he opts to putter around a golf course. At a time when he should be saving money for college tuition, he's out spending foolishly in the pursuit of something he can never achieve—a good golf game. The Holy Grail is still missing; why not try to find that while you're kicking around in the trees looking for yet another lost golf ball.

How to Quit Golf offers the direction, counseling, and tough love that is necessary to rid your life of the most maddening, demanding, and unbalanced game known to man. If you're like everyone else and have had it with the game, but just haven't been able to break free of the shackles that golf has chained to your ankles, this is your bible.

As with all 12-step programs, in order for *How to Quit Golf* to be effective golfers must first admit that perhaps they're not handling the game as well as they could be, and they may possibly have a problem associated with their golfing. Below are questions that the suspecting golfer should ask:

1. When stuck on a highway in bumper-to-bumper traffic, have you ever gotten out of your car to hit shag balls in the median?

2. Have you ever conducted tryouts to determine who your partner will be in the club invitational?

3. Do you wish people would mind their own business about your golfing?

4. Do you play blades?

5. Have you ever been in a passionate embrace, and when the woman you're with said, "I want to see your magic wand," did you run to your car and pull a Ping out of your bag?

6. Have you ever doused yourself in men's cologne to make your husband think you were having an affair, when you were actually at the range getting in some extra work with your irons?

7. Do you envy people who can golf without getting in trouble?

8. Do you tell yourself you can stop golfing any time you want, even though you have a standing, prepaid tee-time every Saturday morning until the day you die?

9. Have you ever made a demonstrative proclamation that you're going to give up the game for good, such as throwing your clubs in a pond and quitting your golf league, only to sneak back at night to retrieve your clubs and join another league across town?

10. Do you own more golf shoes than dress shoes?

11. Have you ever decided to quit golfing for a week, only to find yourself at the driving range within a couple of days, telling yourself it's not really golf if you're not on a course?

12. Do you count going to the driving range with your husband as a night on the town?

13. Given a choice between (a) a week of guilt-free, extramarital sex with the supermodel of your choice, complete with a guarantee that your wife will never find out about it, but all of your buddies will, or (b) a lifetime supply of balls at your local driving range, would you choose b?

14. Have you ever considered throwing yourself in front of the range ball picker due to poor play?

15. When you watch *Caddyshack,* do you turn down the volume and handle all of the dialogue yourself?

Most problem golfers will answer yes to at least seven of these questions.

From the first time the local bully called you a turd-face, you've been overly sensitive to people pointing out your flaws. When it comes to something as personal as your golf game, even the slightest suggestion that you may be losing control is likely to send you into a hissy fit. If someone calls you a no-talent slash, don't take it personally—face it, you probably are. All that we can say in order to ease your pain is that it takes one to know one. In other words, we are not holier than thou, we are thou. And we're here to help. Remember, there is no shame in quitting.

CHAPTER
1

Admit you are powerless over golf—
that your life has become unmanageable.

A dmit it, there are times on the golf course when you get so frustrated by your inability to execute the most elementary shot, that you want to rip your clothes off, run spastically down the fairway screaming obscenities at yourself, jump into a pond, climb out of the water and throw yourself into a bunker, roll around like you're breading a chicken leg, and lie there in tears, praying for crows to come and peck your eyes out so you'll have a reasonable excuse for never playing the game again.

There's no getting around the fact that you are powerless over golf. The game has got you wrapped up tighter than a 100-compression Titleist Balata, and you're caroming through life like a Pinnacle bouncing down a cart path. You've convinced yourself that you could quit if you had a problem, but since you don't have a problem, why should you quit?

Oh, you don't have a problem? Try this: You know the name of everyone in your golf league, and every score you've posted since you switched from forged to cast irons. But you don't know the name of your kid's English teacher, or the score your kid received on his or her most recent spelling test. More than once you've requested, in writing, that your home course erect light towers around the last few greens so you could finish those late evening rounds. For the same reason you'd be more than happy to pay a premium fee for a cart with headlights. Halogen if possible.

Golf owns you. From your logo-emblazoned cap to your spikeless Foot-Joys, golf dictates everything you do, manipulates your emotions, and will eventually call six pallbearers with lower handicaps to your side.

If you're not playing golf, you're thinking about playing golf. When you're not thinking about playing golf, you're thinking you should be thinking about playing golf. Like it or not, your life is spinning out of bounds like a blistered rope-hook off a whippy-shafted, oversized driver.

Problem golfing is a disease, and if you don't think you've been infected, think again. Only a problem golfer would do the things you do, and have the things you have.

Over the past three years you've purchased more than a dozen putters, a half dozen drivers, and sampled twenty-eight different types of golf ball. You're now referring to your stack of first-edition golf instruction manuals as an investment in rare books. You have so many back copies of *Golf Digest, Golf Magazine, Golf Illustrated, Senior Golfer, Golf World, Links, Golf Week, Golf Tips,* and *Southern Golfer,* that your attic has an R-value of 125.

You have a season pass at three different driving

ranges. You can calculate your handicap, to three decimal points, in your head. You actually believe that you can hit a low-draw, or a high-fade, on command, with a two-iron.

You sold your house for the purpose of moving into a community with a cable system that offered the Golf Channel. When that system pulled the Golf Channel, you moved again. You refuse to play miniature golf without your own putter. You listen to golf on the radio, and PGATour.com is your home page.

You religiously watch both the evening and late night *Golf Central* report on the Golf Channel, even though you know that the late night show is a repeat of the evening broadcast. On occasion you have set your alarm to wake you between 1 and 4 A.M. so you could catch an infomercial featuring a "radical new swing technique that will revolutionize the way golf is played." Taping it so you could watch it during daylight hours was never considered.

You don't think twice about skipping work to watch first- and second-round coverage of the Masters, but have never been able to find the time to watch your children in the school play. Your personal collection of artwork begins and ends with an assortment of Leroy Neiman golf posters. You have golf ball racks on your office wall, filled with balls stamped with logos of courses you've never seen, let alone played.

You name your putters. Nothing sweet and simple, like Calamity Jane. No, you name your putters like people name American Kennel Club show dogs: Sir Reginald Ping Backandfrontnine, Most Holy Roller of the 25-footer; Lord Odyssey Von Greensidebunker, Baron of Inside-the-Leather; the Teardrop Earl of Bentsodgrass,

Duke of the Sliding Left-to-Right Downhill Knee-Knocker.

But worst of all, you believe that you can improve your golf game, and that one day other people will consider you to be *a good golfer*. God have mercy on your soul.

Your whole existence centers on one trite activity: hit and chase, hit and chase, hit and chase. Humans call this playing golf. Dogs call this playing fetch. It allows them to run around, first this way, then that, and chase objects that have no inherent value to them. Their tongues wag, they perspire, and they get some fresh air. It's the same thing that happens to you when you golf, though you do it with less grace than the average canine.

What separates man and beast in this instance is that dogs don't dwell on playing fetch, don't read books and magazines about playing fetch, and don't spend gobs of money trying to get better at fetching. Dogs don't sit around after playing fetch rehashing what just happened. They don't bark about how they could've fetched better if it wasn't for the wind, length of the lawn, and their sore paws. Dogs don't harbor deep resentment toward other dogs that are better fetchers than they are. Fetch is just something to do in between doing what they were put on this earth to do: eat, sleep, and occasionally mount your grandmother's leg.

Just like dog, man needs to eat and sleep. We are expected, however, to succeed in an endeavor with more substance than chasing a ball, or humping our grandmother's leg. Regardless of how fun these things can be, both should be out of your system by the time you get a temporary driving permit. In other words, man has been put on this earth to do something productive. It's time to quit golfing and get to it.

No one put a gun to your head and made you golf. It was laid before you, and you grabbed it as fast as you accept conceded putts. Knowing how you got to this state is one thing. Leaving is entirely different. What makes quitting golf so difficult is this: Everyone is powerless over golf because golf is run by the Golf Gods, and there's not a damn thing that you can do about it.

Behold, the power of the gods.

In the much-ballyhooed Showdown at Sherwood match in August of 1999 between David Duval and Tiger Woods, Duval hit a perfect drive, straight down the middle of the sixteenth fairway. His ball came to rest under a boulder that Jack Nicklaus, the course architect, felt would be appropriate to leave in the middle of the sixteenth fairway.

In this example it's obvious that Duval did everything that he was supposed to do, yet he was powerless over golf as to the outcome. As good as David Duval is, after he hit the ball there was nothing he could do. Duval's poor luck is technically referred to as "being boned by the golf gods."

This circumstance could lead one to assume that the golf gods were out to stick it to Duval. This, however, is a myopic view of the big picture. Don't forget that there was a reciprocal beneficiary to Duval's poor luck. How do we know that the golf gods weren't looking out for Tiger Woods?

This is a very plausible scenario. First, Tiger is the anointed savior of the game. The gods can't have their man fall to his archrival on prime-time television. Second, this was a clear signal to Tiger that the gods had his back. Third, the golf gods had already stepped up to the plate for Duval earlier in the year when they helped underwrite the 59 he shot in the final round of the Bob Hope Tournament. For the most part, golf gods like to spread it around.

Sticking a ball under a boulder is a much subtler approach than was used by the gods in days of yore. If the gods had their money on Woods during the heyday of Greek mythology, when gods strutted around like rock stars, treating people with indifference, and sleeping with whomever and whatever they pleased, Duval would have been blasted off the golf course by a lightning bolt, end of story. Today's golf gods go about their work with less dramatic flair than their predecessors; this is the reason Duval wasn't lit up like Ted Bundy during his visit to "Old Sparky."

In examining why we are powerless over golf, the golf god theory carries weight. Who among us hasn't suffered the slings and arrows of outrageous misfortune on the golf course? A ball sliced through a row of trees appears to be heading for the safety of a parallel fairway, only to hit a golf cart and bounce back into the woods. A ball skips a dozen times across a pond, yet falters in its bid to reach land, drowning in six inches of water.

Once you think about it, the presence of golf gods makes perfect sense. Golf can't be this hard; there's got to be something else going on that we just can't see. Much of what happens out on the golf course could be attributable to forces beyond our control. For instance, who could possibly take more than twelve shots on a par three? Nobody can, just the thought is preposterous. It's from here to there; you could almost throw it to the green. You could definitely throw it and make less than a 9. But given the right circumstances, such as a rogue god trying to make a name for himself, nothing is out of the realm of possibility.

Case in point, Tom Weiskopf makes a 13 at the twelfth hole during the 1980 Masters. Even though it is regarded as one of the most difficult and challenging par threes in the world, an eight-year-old should be able to get it home in six. How hard can it be? It's only 155 yards! Bunt it off of the tee, chip it over the creek to behind the green, roll in up onto the putting surface, and three-jack. There, six.

In defense of Weiskopf, it's fair to suggest that had he wanted to make 6 he more than likely could have. At least two times out of three anyway. But throw in some entry-level golf god lurking on the lunatic fringe, and all bets are off. One in the water, two out, three in the water, four out, five in the water, six out, seven in the water, eight out, nine in the water, ten out, eleven on the green, two putts—13.

This is definitely not the work of a human operating unencumbered. The only way to rationalize something like this, lest the victim slide forever into a state of dementia, is to look for some sort of overlord as co-conspirator. Weiskopf should, as most PGA tour players do, acknowledge the existence of golf gods. They recognize the role they play, and realize that it's their world; we're just here to make tee times.

His acceptance of this is the reason he isn't meandering around the streets of Columbus, Ohio, wearing his Ohio State University letter sweater inside out and mumbling, "I could have made nine. I could have made nine. Maybe even eight, but definitely nine."

A collapse of this proportion, to one of the best ball strikers of the last half of the twentieth century, is the stuff of Greek tragedy. The role that the Greek mythology, gods, mortals, and everything in between served in

Greek tragedies correlates directly with the role the golf gods have with the game. They are all over it like white on a Strata. The existence of golf gods also explains why golf is such a crazy game. The Greek gods were as screwed up as the characters in an Aaron Spelling soap opera.

Everything begins with Zeus, the youngest son of a Titan named Cronus. When Zeus grew up, he initiated a hostile takeover and dethroned his old man, making himself CEO of the gods. He tossed off a couple of minor executive-level positions to his brothers Poseidon and Hades, but there was never any confusion over who was calling the shots.

Concluding that he answered to no one, Zeus married his sister, Hera. He fathered many children; Ares, god of war; Eileithyia, goddess of childbirth; Hebe, the goddess of youth; and Hephaestut, the god of fire, just to name a few. Hera, by the way, was not mother to all these kids. Zeus got around. It seems as though Zeus knocked up just about anyone or anything, be they goddesses or mortals or whatnot, and would go to any lengths to get some action.

One story has it that Zeus had the hots for this mortal named Leda, who happened to be married to a Spartan king. That she had a husband meant nothing to Zeus, and apparently not much more to her. Leda also had this thing about waterfowl. Zeus, never one to shy away from a kinky escapade, dressed up like a swan, made goo-goo eyes at Leda, and the two of them got a room.

The tryst resulted in the birth of Polydeuces, and possibly his fraternal twin brother Castor, though Leda's cuckolded husband Tyndareus disputed that. When Castor died, Zeus made him immortal like his brother, and from that point on the two of them spent half their time in the underworld and half with the gods on Mount Olympus. Sort of like a crazy uncle and his longtime companion who summer in the Hamptons and winter in Key West.

To further underscore that the Greek gods were eccentric and self-indulgent whackos, there's the story of Io, daughter of the river god Inachus. She also made Zeus's knees knock, which apparently didn't take much. Word about Io got to Hera. Zeus, fearful that something bad might happen to his latest chippy, changed her into a heifer to protect her from his jealous wife (changing women into barn animals was the Olympian equivalent of setting up a mistress with an apartment and a Neiman Marcus credit card). Suspicious, Hera sent the monster Argus to guard the cow and keep Zeus at arm's length. Then Zeus sent the messenger god Hermes to rescue Io.

Hera, who was fed up, but unable to leave the village and run for senate in an adopted state, decided to torment Io with a gadfly (not the lady who lived across the hall from your first apartment, but a real fly). Io, who apparently was still a heifer at this point, swam across the sea to Egypt, and in doing so set a world swimming record for bovine that stands today. Once again on land, she was restored to a woman, spent a weekend drinking wine and eating feta with Zeus, and ultimately gave him a son, Epaphus. This progeny put Zeus one illegitimate child above the NBA average. All in all, a grossly undisciplined culture, even if it was only mythical.

Today's golf gods have an ancestry of torture, villainy, philandering, narcissism, dirty tricks, and incestuous promiscuity behind them. You wouldn't want these types of people to take care of your geraniums while you were away, and yet they control all of golf. Knowing this, don't you feel stupid for spending so much time trying to figure out why putts that look like they're going to break left actually break to the right?

We can't forget, however, that if the golf gods are responsible for all that goes wrong on the course, then there's a good chance that golf gods also control all that goes right. This quid pro quo of golfing fortunes explains golf's most confounding phenomenon, what we call the *brilliant shot*—the reason to believe.

The brilliant shot is the inexplicable shot that goes exactly where the golfer intended it to go, with total disregard to the skill level of the golfer. The presence of this shot is enough to cloud the mind of golfers into believing that golf nirvana is just around the corner. It lures them back for more, regardless of how bad the rest of the round was. Shrinks call this random reinforcement. You may as well call it crack cocaine.

Feeding on the golfer's weakness, brilliant shots are distributed methodically and purposefully, as though the gods are saying, "Hey, dude, wanna get high?" Golfers get hooked, and therefore create return business.

The brilliant shot is usually presented in three forms:

1. *The perfect drive.* This shot is always, without exception, followed by the statement "Where's that been all day? That's how I was hitting 'em on the range." That shot has been on the range all day because that's where the golf gods keep them until it's time to mess with someone's skull. Then they toss it out there just to watch how the recipient golfer reacts. The gods are never disappointed.

2. *The chip-in from off the green.* Many a golfer will vocalize how he was "owed that one" by the golf gods. The golf gods owe nothing to anyone. Especially some chop who believes his drive into the woods, his insistent slice, his cold tops off the tee, his approach shots into ponds, and his chronic three-putting are the result of him being in disfavor in the eyes of the overseers of the game. Golfers are given a chip-in by the gods because they rejoice in seeing angry men spend good money to scrape it around, and piss and moan all afternoon. They want you to come back.

3. *A birdie on the number 1 handicap hole.* This occurrence is doubly evil. First, like many other euphoriant drugs, it provides a short-term sense of happiness, and deludes the golfer into thinking she can always feel this good. Second, a birdie on a tough hole will likely win a skin. Now the golfer is not only euphorically delusional, she's got extra walking-around money in her pocket. Cash she will undoubtedly use to feed her Jones, with either a down payment on a new driver, or a trip to the range and an extra large bucket.

Most of the time brilliant shots will occur over the final three holes of a round, and therefore will be fresh in the golfer's mind as he leaves the course. Without the incidence of these brilliant shots, golf would have the social and commercial impact of feather bowling.

Given that there's no difference between the score of 103 and the 101 that is the result of the brilliant shot, it can be concluded that these shots happen for the sole purpose of golfer retention. So therefore, not only do the golf gods oversee the game, they are the enablers of the game. Pushers if you will.

They use brilliant shots as an opiate, and prey on the central nervous system of naive golfers. If you've ever bent a shaft across your head and asked, "Why do I continue to play this stupid game?" now you know—you're a junkie. As with all addictions there are health risks that come with golf. After long-term exposure to these sporadic shots, the problem golfer's nerve cells begin to degenerate. This results in the golfer becoming physically dependent on an external supply of these shots.

The problem golfer will spend more and more time on the practice range. She'll pound ball after ball attempting to develop the skills believed necessary to hit brilliant shots of her own fruition on the course. She will become proficient at hitting almost any shot she can envision while on the range, but under no circumstances will she ever be able to duplicate on the course what she does on the practice tee.

Long-term dependency on these brilliant shots can turn into a physical illness and central nervous system disorder. Many can recall seeing a fellow golfer out on the practice range after dark, grinding away, trying to find it. As a cart boy leads her back to the clubhouse, she's seen twitching and talking to herself: "I've got to hold parallel at the top. Parallel at the top, pointed down the line. Parallel at the top, pointed down the line. At the top, down the line." At this stage her family doesn't even want her.

Most problem golfers will claim that they are powerless over golf because they *are* powerless over golf. They assert that they have no control over the time and money they spend on the game. Their devotion to the game, and their collection of silly golf stuff, is out of their hands because they are nothing more than a puppet on the end of the golf gods' string. The problem golfer will defer all responsibility of her affliction to an outside agency—the golf gods. Believing firmly that since the gods have their fingers on the triggers of everything golf related, all golfers are powerless. So not only have the lives of problem golfers become unmanageable, the problem golfer is as crazy as hitting a one-iron out of a green side bunker.

When Neil Armstrong set foot on the moon, he said, "That's one small step for man, one giant leap for mankind." Two years later Alan Shepard would hit a golf ball on the moon with a makeshift six-iron. We can do many things, overcome enormous obstacles, and achieve heroic successes, like putting a man on the moon, but we haven't figured out a way to quit golf—until now.

You should consider Chapter One a small step that will build into the giant leap of quitting golf. No chapter on its own can do the job, but in concert, the twelve steps of *How to Quit Golf* will release you from the earthlike gravity that has held you under the oppressive nature of golf for all of these years.

CHAPTER
2

Come to believe that a power greater than yourself can restore you to sanity.

Golfers across the world, from the PGA Tour professional to the weekend hacker, wear the message of their faith around their wrists. W.W.J.D.? bracelets abound, giving golfers guidance and strength, helping them make decisions when in a bind.

Perhaps an errant tee-shot has left him blocked out by trees. She may discover her approach has resulted in a fried-egg lie in a bunker. He may face a moment of truth, such as whether or not to reveal to playing partners that he whiffed back in the woods. Or, perish the thought, she's got a fifth putt that's a knee-knocker.

During moments of crisis, anguish, or moral temptation, golfers ask themselves W.W.J.D.? These bracelets are a telltale sign that the wearer has a strong belief in a power greater than themselves. Jack Nicklaus is that greater power. They ask themselves, "What Would Jack Do?"

Perhaps you were thinking of someone else?

Perhaps you were thinking that during times of personal strife one should ask, "What Would Jesus Do?" True, he has a good reputation as a reliable higher power. Millions of people look to him as their savior, their guiding light. Word is he can even get the job done when it calls for delivering people from evil and temptation. That's all fine and dandy, but truth be told, when it comes to issues pertaining to golf, it's better to ask, "What Would Jack Do?"

The problem we have with asking Jesus what he would do lies in what his answer might be. For instance, you may find yourself in the left rough, under a tree, about 130 yards from the green, which is fronted by a small pond. You have no idea what to do, but you do know you don't have this shot. So you ask Jesus for a little guidance (this may in fact be in violation of Rule 8-1 regarding the asking of advice, unless Jesus is either your playing partner or caddy, which we would tend to doubt).

So you ask Jesus what to hit in the above situation, and he says "Driver." Therein lies the problem. The guy can walk on water, so it would be logical to surmise that he has no concerns as to getting his ball across the pond. He probably doesn't even see the pond. But you do, you see every hazard, which may be the reason you land in so many of them, but we digress.

Additionally, he's Jesus. He can hit driver, putter, three-iron, or even a tire iron for that matter, and hit the green, probably hole-out if he puts any thought to it. You, on the other hand, are not Jesus. And though his guidance and strength may get people through a variety of daily perils, it may be best to remember that Jesus was a carpenter, not a golfer, and he may have no more clue as to what you should hit than you do.

This of course brings us back to Jack, the greater

power in golf. The greater power is wise. The greater power is experienced. The greater power has walked down that fairway of righteousness, and can lead us through the primary rough of darkness. The greater power has also won eighteen major championships, more than any other greater power known to man. If we could only speak to Jack, he could surely return us to sanity.

In order to appreciate fully this greater power and all that he represents, we must seek his insight. We must flock to him and summon his wisdom. We must feel the presence of his greatness and beg to have it thrust upon us. We must endure arduous journeys, which could involve numerous flight delays. We must weather severe hardships, such as watching the greater power suffer through the inadequacies of his pro-am playing partners (there but for the grace of God go we).

Over the centuries many people from different cultures have resorted to pilgrimage in an effort to find enlightenment and spiritual fulfillment. This, by the way, is different from making a pilgrimage to a resort, which is one of the reasons you need this book in the first place. Though one may argue, "But I visited a resort with a Jack Nicklaus Signature golf course, is that not the same? Is that not akin to traveling to Mecca, or at least to an upscale subdivision of Mecca?"

No, you moron. Even traveling to Muirfield Village, somehow squirreling onto the course, and getting in all eighteen before being summarily booted from the grounds is not what needs to happen. That is the equivalent of the alcoholic seeking sanctuary among the pristine mountaintops of Golden, Colorado, and then taking in a tour of the Adolph Coors Brewing Company.

In seeking out a power greater than us, one that possesses insight much deeper and clearer than we could possibly fathom, we must go directly to the source. We must go to Jack. We must speak to Jack.

A case could be made that in order to find religion, one need not "do lunch" with the Almighty. True, but a brief conversation over a grilled chicken Caesar and ice tea would provide an opportunity to clear up a lot of questions. Besides, God isn't strolling the fairways of the Senior PGA Tour. He isn't out there banging balls on the range. In other words, Jack is more accessible than God, though not by much.

It seems apparent that the majority of golfers are true believers. For those that aren't, well, we can't save everybody. Believing that this greater power can restore sanity, however, is more of a leap of faith. Golfers must have no doubt that if the greater power guides them in a direction, that path will lead to a better life. It is our firm and unwavering assertion that a better life can only be achieved without golf. The skeptic in all of us will noodle this for a moment and ask, "Well, what was life like before golf?" Good question.

In response to a similar query, "What's it like to be a Beatle?" George Harrison once responded, "What's it like not to be a Beatle?" The problem golfer faces the same dilemma: What's it like not to be a slicing, chunking, shanking, three-whacking hack?

Many of us have known only golf. Golf was introduced to us when we were young, often by well-meaning but poorly misguided parents. These parents unwittingly had become mesmerized by the game, and failed to consider the potential long-term consequences. Golfing parents are the same type of parents who freely puffed cigarettes in their homes, not realizing that secondhand smoke was a group-A carcinogen.

For these types of golfers the game has been with them their entire lives. They can't remember when they didn't play golf. These "born-into-the-game" golfers have no pre-golf reference point. They have no understanding that life itself is possible without golf.

They are like the children born into communism. They know little of freedom and Western culture, other than it offers an endless supply of blue jeans, Coca-Cola, and video games. Born-into-the-game golfers don't know what it's like not to be a golfer. They don't know there is another world out there. A world free from complex issues such as graphite or steel, balata or surlyn, cast or forged. These golfers are the hardest to reach, the hardest to save.

Then there are golfers who survived childhood only to succumb to peer pressure during adolescence. This country has an ugly history of losing children to golf. These lost souls, looking for a place to fit in, innocently accept an invitation to the driving range from the cool kids in school. Thinking golf will be their ticket to the in crowd, they go along, only to become hopelessly hooked.

Many of these peer pressure golfers have flashbacks to life before golf. Many can recollect a simpler time in their life when there were no battles for Saturday and Sunday morning tee-times. When family vacations weren't structured around the quality of nearby golf courses. When there was something other than golf on TV during weekend afternoons.

The most tragic, and pitiful, of all golfers is the latent golfer. This is the poor, dumb bastard who makes it into adulthood without the stranglehold of golf around his neck, then takes up the game late in life for business purposes, believing that somehow through golf he can further his career. This idea is as sound as trying to win the heart of a Hollywood starlet by stalking and attempting to kill the President.

The latent golfer's biggest mistake is in not understanding the hierarchy of golf in the business world. There is a direct correlation between how much money you make and how good a golfer you are. All the best nonprofessional golfers are salesmen. Salesmen make the most money. Knowing this, companies hire good golfers to be their salesmen. The downside to this is that salesmen have the highest incidence of becoming problem golfers, but corporate America could care less. What's one more life lost to golf when quarterly earnings are at stake?

Another major error in judgment by the latent golfer is in believing that he can take up the game late in life and become a decent golfer, quickly propelling himself into the world of sales, thinking that once in sales he will be able to make almost as much money as Jack himself, therefore justifying taking up the game for business purposes.

This is completely erroneous. Lets make this perfectly clear—no one is any good at this game; some people just play more than others. The latent golfer has a better chance of ascending to the British throne than he does developing any skill for the game. Having said that, it's important to immediately squelch the counter argument: that salesmen always lose to their clients, and therefore the latent golfer would actually have an advantage in sales because he sucks.

Forget about that client golf nonsense. There is no such thing as client golf. That went out with three-martini lunches and golf shoes with kilts. People aren't stupid. Any buyer, purchasing agent, or person of equivalent corporate standing isn't shameless enough to accept a salesman caving in to him on the golf course for the purposes of getting his hands on something as trivial as a five-dollar Nassau. Anyone trying to pull that stunt finds himself on the losing end of any deal, even with the low bid.

People are shameless enough, however, to accept a round of golf at an exclusive country club, a dozen balls, a constant flow of food and beverages, and a shirt. Two shirts if the club has recently held, or will be holding, a major championship and logo'd merchandise is available. Because of this unabashedly blatant acceptance of golf and related items as the official currency of graft, salesmen routinely take their clients three-ways, plus presses, just to remind buyers of their lowly place on the golf and wealth food chain.

Though the members from each of the above groups have varying degrees of exposure to the game of golf, and carry different types of baggage, 99 percent of them are flat-out bonkers. Their only saving grace is that, especially if they saw the 1986 Masters, they believe in a greater power. They may not, however, know that they are flat-out bonkers.

A big hurdle in convincing problem golfers they are insane is in defining what insanity is, and that whatever it is they've got buckets full of it. In answering this question, it may be easier to explore feelings and behavior best associated with forms of mental illness. In *Moby Dick,* Herman Melville gave us this glimpse of madness:

The lightning flashes through my skull; mine eyeballs
ache and ache; my whole beaten brain seems as be-
headed, and rolling on some stunning ground.

For those of you who find Melville to be as confounding as playing from the tips, here's an example from the
front tees: In *National Lampoon's Vacation,* Chevy
Chase, who is married, is standing poolside about to go
skinny-dipping with Christie Brinkley, who is not his wife.
He is saying the following,

This is crazy, this is crazy, this is crazy.

Either of these hit a nerve? If this is the way you felt
the last time you missed a two-foot putt, rope-hooked a
three-iron out of bounds while playing conservative off
the tee, or bounced a brand-new ball into a pond while
trying to lay up—you're insane, end of story.

It's the feeling that even if you tried you couldn't do
any worse that what you've just done. Such as toeing a
driver, and having the ball ricochet off a tee-marker
back into your face, breaking your nose—culminating in
a penalty of two strokes, in medal play, after which the
ball must be played as it lies (Rule 19-2b), or if in match
play, the loss of the hole (Rule 19-2a). As Ken Venturi
would say, "Jimmy [Jim Nance], he couldn't hit that
shot again if he took a bag of balls down there and tried
all week."

From the outside it's easy to see that golfers are disturbed. A big hurdle is for golfers themselves to come to
grips with it. If you're crazy, and you're crazy all day long,
how the hell do you know you're nuts? If a guy carries a
mouse in his pocket, rubbing its head day in and day out,

and he's been doing it for ten years, even though the mouse has been dead for nine years and eleven months, why would that guy consider his behavior odd? He wouldn't; to him it's perfectly normal. From that guy's perspective people who aren't stroking a dead mouse in their pocket are the ones who need to stay after school for special attention.

If pressed to present one piece of evidence that golfers are indeed mental, we would offer the club-less swing. Anywhere, anytime, golfers can be found swinging a club that isn't there—in elevators, at desks, in hallways, on street corners, in courtrooms, gyms, churches, grocery stores, theaters, airplanes, restaurants, classrooms, funeral homes, pools, saunas, sitting on the toilet, and even while having sex. Always playing with it, always under the assumption that no one is watching. Just like no one sees them pick their noses while driving down the highway. Be it a full swing or a waggle, the club-less swing is the mouse in the golfer's pocket.

This type of behavior leads us to believe that golfers swim in the same kind of gene pool that spawned such luminaries as Mark David Chapman, King George III, and whoever developed the USGA handicap system. The truth is that golfers are inherently insane. As the old saying goes, you can't choose your relatives, and golf's bloodline is as inbred as the House of Windsor.

Golf's embryonic stage took place during the 1400s in Scotland. A country, it should be noted, whose only other contribution to international sport has been *tossing the caber*. The game that we are familiar with started to come together in the mid 1500s. To understand fully why golf is the dwelling of madmen, all one needs to examine is what was going on in the kingdom during the time golf first raised its ugly head.

In 1542 a baby girl named Mary Stuart was born in Linlithgow, Scotland. Her father, James V, died immediately after her birth, and at six days old she became queen. You know her as Mary Queen of Scots, who among other things has been credited as being the first woman golfer. She married quite young, around two or three years of age, to Prince Edward of England, her half-brother. This marriage was subsequently annulled by the Scottish Parliament, which resulted in a war with England. Don't read too much into this, almost everything the Scots did in the sixteenth century resulted in a war with England. It served to keep both economies strong, and provided a constant flow of young widows for the bluebloods to escort about.

After the Scots got their collective asses handed to them at a place called Pinkie, Mary, just five years old and still the queen of Scotland, was shipped off to France to be raised. A variety of reasons are cited, none more plausible than she just tired of haggis and tripe. At age sixteen she would marry a Frenchman, some bloke referred to as the Dauphin, who would become king of France. Sadly, his reign lasted for about as long as it takes to play a quick nine.

In Mary's absence, St. Andrews Golf Club was founded, which was reason enough to head home, and in 1561 she moved back to rule Scotland. Before she left France, however, she placed an eternal curse on French golf. The effect of which was recently felt by Jean Van de Velde at the 1999 British Open, which was held on Mary's former turf.

In 1565 Mary got hitched once more. The lucky fellow this time was Scottish nobleman Henry Stuart, aka Lord Darnley, aka Mary's cousin. Wasting little time in asserting his perceived power as spouse of the queen, he ordered the grisly murder of Mary's secretary and advisor, David Rizzio. Apparently Darnley felt Rizzio stood in the way of him becoming King for Life, so he had him snatched away from a dinner he was having with Mary, hacked to death with daggers, and thrown into a courtyard.

Early in 1567, Stuart, who was rumored to be a bit of a cad, as well as a self-absorbed megalomaniac, got his comeuppance and was bumped off. Reports on his untimely demise are cloudy; he was either strangled or blown up. Whatever the cause of death, more than a few people pointed fingers at Mary and this guy named James Hepburn, Fourth Earl of Bothwell. Within days of Henry's murder Mary was found out on the links, trying to get a few holes in before dark. This is where the phrase "When the going gets tough, the tough go golfing" originated.

With total disregard to public perception, Hepburn divorced his wife and kidnaped Mary before Stuart's legs stiffened up. Mary, who once again found herself technically single, decided to give the marriage thing one more shot. In May of 1567 Mary, who was Catholic, and Hepburn, who was not, were wed in a Protestant church.

The marriage, particularly the venue, irritated the hell out of a bunch of Scottish noblemen. A war ensued—no surprise there—and the victorious noblemen forced Mary to send Bothwell's fourth earl packing. In addition, they requested that Mary abdicate the throne and turn the whole shooting match over to her thirteen-month-old son, who was proclaimed King James VI of Scotland on

July 24, 1567. All of this and Mary had barely reached her twenty-fifth birthday.

Over the next few years Mary tried unsuccessfully to get the throne back. Realizing it was a lost cause, she sought refuge in England, which at the time was under the leadership of yet another one of her cousins, Queen Elizabeth I. As soon as Mary set foot in England, Liz made her prisoner for life—a life that ended badly in 1587, when Elizabeth ordered that Mary's head be lopped off during halftime of a local rugby scrum.

The point of all this is to highlight what was going on when golf was young and impressionable. Suffice to say, if your family was like this when you were growing up, you'd be a nut basket too. That golf has gotten this far without hours upon hours of therapy is testament to its inner strength. It also goes to a long way to explaining why the game has evolved into such a miserably manipulative and spiteful institution, not unlike haute couture fashion.

This once again brings us full circle to W.W.J.D.?

Jack, being the greater power that he is, knows all of this. He knows the history of the game. He knows how it got started and how it developed into the haven of psychosis that it has become. Jack knows of the dread and uncertainty golfers experience. He understands the emotional perils of being a golfer, and the mental hopscotch that goes on in the head of anyone with a club in his hand.

To be delivered from a life riddled with chaos, to a life of peaceful serenity, one must seek Jack out, and ask for his guidance and strength to do the right thing. Once the golfer has bowed before Jack as a penitent, misguided soul, once his transgressions have been confessed, and he has borne witness to the fact he is a problem golfer, then, and only then, may the golfer ask, "How can I save myself?"

Jack will undoubtedly respond, "Quit the game."

CHAPTER
3

***Make a decision to turn your will and
your life over to the pursuit of something
other than golf.***

If you're serious about quitting golf, then you're going to
have to get serious about doing something else. By now
you're beginning to realize how all-encompassing the
pursuit of the game has become in your life. Removing
golf will create a vast cavity that will need to be filled. If
not, the pain will be too intense, and you'll find yourself
back on the course in no time.

There's an old joke that doesn't go like this, but it
should:

Q: Why do you play golf?

A: Because it feels good when I stop.

In order for you to stop for good, there needs to be a
change in your behavior. The following exercises are designed to loosen the grip that golf has around your throat.
By admitting to yourself, then others, that golf has become a problem, you can begin to explore other avenues
of leisure activity.

Essential exercises for the problem golfer as he heads
into recovery:

- Each day make a statement that you will not golf that day. If you played, you wouldn't play well anyway, so what's the point?

- Go to at least one meeting a day. This should be a meeting that you would normally have blown off in order to play golf. A good start may be a parent-teacher conference or that annual review with your boss you keep postponing.

- Once a day, break a club across your knee. For many of you this will be the first time you've broken a club that hasn't done anything to deserve it.

- Surf through the channels on your TV, forcing yourself to slide right through the Golf Channel without stopping to see if anybody is posting a good number at the Hootie and the Blowfish Invitational.

- Talk to another problem golfer about her recovery program. It's good to know that you're not the only freak in the circus.

Once you've blended these activities into your daily routine, it's time to explore other opportunities. The world is full of glorious diversions and avocations; get off your duff and go find one.

What you choose as a replacement for golf will initially be determined by your state of mind. If this sudden withdrawal from the game has left you nervous and puzzled, it's best to start with something easy. One of the following will be a good place to begin: stamp collecting, bird-watching, needlepoint, remote-control toys, board games, baking, model trains, crossword puzzles, wood carving, a yo-yo, checkers, card tricks, or paper airplanes.

Your initial response to this list may be that all of those things are stupid and boring. Yes, they are. But the psyche of someone who has recently quit the game is extremely fragile. Delving into anything more complicated could result in a devastating failure, and then the recovering golfer would be lost forever. To start, it's recommended that one of the above hobbies be mastered. This should take about a week, given how childish they are, but maybe longer for a golfer. Then something more interesting can be attempted.

Once the groundwork has been laid, it's time to discover a second calling. At this stage you want to find something that is challenging and rewarding, but not anything that could be as habit forming and destructive as golf. After talking with experts in the field of addiction treatment and recovery, we can recommend the following pastimes for the problem golfer, each sharing certain elements or characteristics with golf. Not unlike a nicotine patch for people attempting to quit smoking, these pursuits can help ease the transition away from the game.

One other item needs to be mentioned: quitting golf should not be attempted cold turkey. It's much too dangerous and the results usually have a tragic ending. Those people you've seen standing on street corners, wearing plastic bags, oversized hats and two left shoes, yelling at garbage cans and streetlights, directing traffic and proclaiming they have seen the end and that it's near, those are people who tried to quit golf cold turkey.

Gardening. Getting involved with horticulture is an excellent way to remove golf from your life. The uplifting feeling one gets from nurturing a plant from seedling to maturity is far greater than the brief thrill of dropping a twelve-foot putt for triple-bogey.

There are many similarities between golf and gardening. Both are outside activities, but can be moved indoors as it gets colder. In the winter golfers go into domed driving ranges. Gardeners go into glass houses.

You move around dirt while gardening; you move around dirt while getting out of a bunker. Gardeners are always planting things; golfers often plant a putter in the green after consecutive three-putts. Gardeners are always around grass, trees, shrubs, and water. Golfers are always in grass, trees, shrubs, and water.

Once some basic skills are developed, ornamental gardening can be explored. This type of landscape architecture features the molding and shaping of plants. By venturing into this style of gardening you will use many of the skills you picked up from golf, such as slicing, hacking, chopping, scraping, carving, chunking, and topping.

The downside to gardening is that if you screw up, things can die. Many problem golfers will not be able to handle the fact that they've killed something. Though golfers have killed a round, killed a drive, and killed a beer, none of these things was animate before the golfer got his hands on them. So gardening, as good as an alternative to golf as it is, should only be selected by someone who can deal with the idea that death among plants is a daily hazard.

Bowling. At first blush this seems absurd—bowling and golf share nothing in common. For the most part this is true. Bowling is always contested indoors, except for lawn bowling. The minimum age for that activity is seventy-eight, so it is useless to us. Besides, if you're still golfing at age seventy-eight, God bless you. Hell, if you're doing anything at age seventy-eight, God bless you.

Bowling is confined, noisy, and simpleminded. But what it lacks in sophistication it more than makes up for with structure. Bowling is a very good sport—well, sport is a stretch, but a very good substitute for golf because it gives the problem golfer focus.

The best thing about bowling is that you never lose your ball. No matter how bad your shot, you can be certain that the ball will come back. How great is that? No hiking through the woods, fishing around in streams and ponds, searching endlessly in rough and brush. Just fling it down the lane and, regardless of the result, it'll show up right next to you in a moment or two.

Without the enormous financial pressure of losing yet another ball, the bowler can just deal with the matter at hand, knocking down those pins. No wind, rain, uphill, side hill, or downhill lies to confuse—just fling that sucker down the alley and whatever happens, happens. Even in the unlikely event that the ball jumps lanes, it will still be returned.

How many times have golfers lost a ball after launching it into the wrong fairway? Balls in opposing fairways are consistently pocketed by people other than their owners. But in bowling, no matter how horrific your shot, you're going to get the ball back. The guy on the next lane over isn't going to crotch your Brunswick.

Bowling also builds camaraderie. Bowlers all sit close to one another, don't venture off in different directions after playing their shot, and have a lot of downtime. This enables them to have in-depth conversations over such intimate subjects as the weight of their balls.

Last, and most important, bowling the perfect game is

achievable. It happens all of the time. Check the sports section of any big-city daily and you'll find a list of people who have rolled a perfect game. Then look for the list of people who've played a perfect round of golf. It should be in the same section where the stories on permanent world peace and cars that run on water can be found.

The perfect game of golf doesn't exist, but every golfer strives for perfection. This is yet another reason golfers are so messed up—they're constantly trying to do something that can't be done. Proving Fermat's Last Theorem was an uphill, two-inch putt compared to the perfect round of golf. Bowling paints perfection in a nice, big round number: 300. Bowling defines it, embraces it, and rewards it. Bowling gives the problem golfer the target he seeks and the direction he so desperately needs. The shirts and shoes are funny looking, but who are golfers to complain about bad clothing?

Jogging. This will immediately draw stiff resistance from most problem golfers. If they wanted to take up jogging, they would have gone out for cross-country in high school. Jogging, damn it, is work, and work is not what golf is all about. Golf is about leisure, pacing yourself, tempo, concentration, and finesse. Jogging is about sweating, shin splints, sore muscles, and commitment.

Yet, when examined closely, jogging and golf share common characteristics. Both activities create perspiration, although golfers will only sweat if it's ninety-eight degrees and humid. Both take place over large areas, though golfers cruise around in carts with automatic steering, over cushy grass, and joggers pound their knees into chalk dust on concrete. Both can raise heartbeats, but golfers tend to get their hearts racing only if they have an easy putt to win a skin, probably too infrequent to offer any health benefits. If golfers can get past the idea that jogging is good for them they may buy into it.

Another co-characteristic of golfing and jogging is the endorphin rush. Joggers swear by this natural substance that is pumped throughout the brain. Acting as a neuro-transmitter, it brings the jogger to a state of euphoria. This is the same type of feeling that golfers get after hitting a brilliant shot. The problem is that there is no sure-fire way to duplicate this feeling on the course. The golfer goes days, weeks, or even months without that needed boost. It's the root of his problems.

Joggers, on the other hand, can just slip on a pair of Nikes and trot around the block a few times whenever they need a fix. Jogging could be looked at as something like a methadone clinic for problem golfers. The rush they need is there, though channeled through a different delivery system. By taking up jogging, the golfer will be doing something that benefits herself and her family.

Before you trade in your Softspikes for waffle soles, be sure to check with your doctor. The most exercise golfers get is chasing after the guy in the adjoining fairway who pocketed their slice. Once the doctor gives the go-ahead, you'll to want to start slow. From the back porch to the front porch will be good; then call it a day. Eventually you'll be able to run around a golf course. But take it easy—we're not trying to kill you, just rehabilitate you.

Tennis. Forget it—tennis is as dead as the gutta-percha ball and hickory shafts.

Day Trading. There's nothing like day trading for pure adrenaline flow. Knocking in a mid-iron from 150 yards for eagle? Not close. Hole-in-one? Fleeting. The idea that you can take all of your money, borrow a bunch more from someone you don't know, and start buying and selling stocks is the essence of capitalism.

From nine-thirty in the morning to four o'clock in the afternoon, EST, you can outsmart those pansies from Goldman Sachs and Janus as they stumble all over themselves like the Keystone Kops of portfolio management. What's the most money you've ever won on a golf course, $20, $50, or $100? Maybe even $1,000 in some wild-ass pare-mutual Calcutta? Chump change compared to the gobs of money you can make by jumping on the mistakes the big boys make. We're talking American Dream–type money here.

You'll be screaming stuff like "Don't bring that sissy-boy crap in my house, Fidelity. Who's your daddy, J.P. Morgan, who's your daddy?" Day trading will allow you to amass a quick fortune in front of a computer terminal while scoffing at the most brilliant and seasoned minds in the investment world. You'll be pulling the trigger on market-shattering deals in no time. All from the comfort of your self-styled trading bunker in your basement.

As the earning-less stocks that you and your chatroom buddies are buying rocket into the stratosphere, reporters from major financial periodicals and broadcast networks will clamor outside your home. They'll beg for interviews, promising cover stories and prime-time exposure. Within months you'll be able to buy the golf course you used to play, just so you can honestly say, "I own that course."

Yes, day trading can be your deliverance from the evils of golf, sweeping it out of your life and replacing it with the type of freedom that can only come with not having to balance your checkbook. Through day trading you will see that golf is a vacant avocation, void of moral, social, and intellectual, not to mention monetary, remuneration. Only day trading can bring you the financial security, inner peace, and spiritual serenity that to this point has been the exclusive enclave of third-generation money.

The only possible downside to day trading is the correction. This is somewhat similar, though with much graver repercussions, to the wind gusting in your face just as you've hit a shot over a body of water. It happens this way: Some buttoned-down Wall Street analyst announces at lunchtime on CNBC that the company whose helium-inflated stock you've remortgaged your house and margined your children's college fund to buy will never make any money, that said company has in fact falsified every document they ever filed with the SEC.

As blood begins to squirt out from under your fingernails as you squeeze your mouse and pound your keyboard, the analyst continues. He reports that as of three days ago the founder of the company and all of his executive team blew out their entire stock positions. They are rumored to be buck naked, drinking Dom Perignon like it is Gatorade, riding stolen dirt bikes, and wildly humping European hookers on some remote island that doesn't have an extradition treaty with anybody.

While you, and every other jester who thinks stock picking is something you can do in between loads of laundry, frantically try to dump what's left of the stock in the wake of a mass exodus by day traders across the globe, the analyst concludes his remarks. He mentions that though this development will cripple a lot of individual investors, institutional players have long seen it coming. Most are short the stock.

At this point you will learn a valuable lesson about market liquidity—or in your case, illiquidity. Margins calls, by the way, are a bitch.

Croquet. OK, so it's generally played by old men in white shorts who don't have the legs for it. It does, however, have one element that is desperately lacking in golf—defense. In golf there is no way for you to stop your opponent. When he has it going, there isn't anything you can to do to slow him down. But croquet has an equalizer: the send.

In croquet, any time you hit your opponent's ball you get to the send the guy. Place your ball next to his, your foot on your ball, smash into your ball with a standard-issue mallet head, and send your opponent's ball into oblivion.

Just think if you could do that in golf. If marking the ball was illegal, a player could try to hit her opponent's ball. If successful, then the player would get to tee-up her opponent's ball and send it where she may. Say you're down three shots heading into the seventeenth green, and you nudge your opponent's ball. Tee it up and whack it into the pond two fairways away—new ball game.

Oh well, that will never happen. Even if it did, you can barely manage to hit the hole, which is twice as large as a ball. You may as well quit the game and take up croquet.

Racquetball. Makes tennis look like the X-Games.

Fishing. Like gardening, fishing takes place outside, embracing nature and the elements. Both golfing and fishing provide sufficient time for male bonding, lend themselves to great amounts of boasting and exaggeration, and almost command that beer be drunk as the event unfolds.

Unlike jogging, fishing takes time, lots of time. Even if you were to run a marathon, you'd finish well before the time it takes to get in a good day of fishing. The reason fishing takes so much time is that you can't see where the fish are. It's like trying to find your wife in a shopping mall. You know that she's in there, but you haven't the foggiest idea where she might be. You could spend hours just trying to find your wife. Same with trying to find fish. Since the object is to catch them, not just find them, fishing can easily fill the gap created when you quit golf.

Fishing is more complex than golf for that very reason. You know where practically everything is on the golf course. The targets are even marked with those little flags, leaving practically nothing to the imagination (which makes it even more ludicrous that golf is so damn hard). With fishing, you're clueless. No idea where the little bastards are. That's why fish finders were developed, to give fishermen a fighting chance, and to give them something material to brag to their buddies about.

In addition to fish finders, equipment options abound. Problem golfers will be humbled by the amount and variety of equipment fishermen hoard. You think your collection of a dozen or so putters is impressive? There's not a fisherman worth his salt that doesn't have at least twice that many rods in his truck alone. Believe you're in a league of your own because your shag bag contains over three hundred golf balls? Wait until you see a 500-slot tackle box, filled to capacity, which will be just one of many tackle boxes the serious fisherman has with him at all times.

If you think trying to choose which golf ball to buy is laborious, spend an afternoon in a sports mega store. The golf section will look like a pimple on the butt of the fishing department. The bait area alone offers a selection process as difficult to understand as a five-way Nassau with automatic two-down presses and carryover skins. Spinner bait, crank bait, floating bait, sinking bait, and live bait—and you don't have the faintest notion which ones will work and which ones won't because you've never seen a fish eat.

Trying to catch fish is like trying to feed kids. You place what you think they'll eat in an area you think they'll be. Even if they do show up, however, the chances of them eating what you're offering is remote. This is why fishing is such a great alternative to golf. You still won't be able to do what you're trying to do, and it will frustrate you to no end, but this time it's not your fault. It's not like you need to break a rod over your knee in disgust. You're dealing with the unreasonable idiosyncrasies of an entire species, a lesser developed one at that.

Fishing and golf also share the rich ancestry of being developed into a gentlemen's pastime by the Scots. The oldest fishing club in existence is in Ellem, not too far down the road from St. Andrews. Given the cultural heritage of Scotland, it's easy to understand the mental makeup of those who fish. The world's sanest fisherman makes Jesper Parnevik look like Ben Hogan. The only saving grace fishermen have is that after being away from home all day they can claim they were out catching supper. Golfers bring nothing to the table.

Sex. This is quite possibly the perfect offset to golf. Golf can invigorate the mind and body; sex can invigorate the mind and body. Golf is a lifelong pursuit; sex is a lifelong pursuit. Each feature some of the same components: holes, balls, bags, shafts, heads, hazards, and whips. OK, maybe whips aren't used as much in golf as they should be, but it's hard to argue that they don't have a place.

When you're beginning to learn the game, especially if you get involved with a league, it's not unusual to play with a lot of people. You can play as a single, double, threesome, or foursome. Once you settle in and get comfortable with one partner you may play together for a long time. After a while you'll discover each other's strengths and weaknesses, and you'll both want to improve the quality of your performance and focus on the score. If your partner does one thing, you may want to do another. As you become more proficient, you'll develop certain strategies, such as being above or below the hole. All of this is also true of golf.

With sex, as in golf, reservations are accepted, but both are fun on the spur of the moment. You can do both with people you know, or with people you don't. Participants in each activity have great admiration for length, and anything oversized is coveted. Creativity is rewarded, especially in tight areas. Pace of play is a major concern, though one activity encourages speed while the other frowns upon it.

By forsaking golf for sex you will be able to spend more time with your family, or possibly start one. You'll also find time on your hands since sex, no matter how attentive you are to detail, shouldn't take as long to complete as a round of golf. You should also be getting more rest, since more than likely you'll just roll over and go to sleep when you're finished.

The transition from golf to sex should be easy since they share much of the same language. While engaging in sex, you and your partner will be using many phrases that are commonplace in golf, for instance:

"Never up, never in."

"Wow, when did you get the new equipment?"

"Down, down, get down."

"What hole are we on?"

"Not there, oh no, Don't go in there."

"The head on that thing is huge."

"I'd sure like to do that hole over again."

"You might want to change your ball position."

"How stiff is your shaft?"

"Looks like about six inches, maybe a bit more."

"I'm just going to run it up between those two mounds."

"The hole opens up from this angle."

"Bite, damn it, bite."

"I can only get in a few more holes, then I've got to be heading home."

"What do you mean you're done playing?"

"I always do better on the backside."

"It's harder than the seventeenth at St. Andrews."

Initially we are attracted to both golf and sex for the same reason: It seems like fun. We read about it in books, see pictures of it, and maybe even get a peek at friends doing in it. We think that this is something we'd like to try. Both come easy at first, expectations are low, and just participating is enough for most.

The best reason to replace golf with sex is that you don't need to be good at sex in order to have fun. You can have absolutely zero sexual aptitude and still have the time of your life. Don't know how to get Tab A into Slot

B? Who cares? Just fiddle around with it and sooner or later you'll achieve the desired results. Best of all, there's practically no wrong way to have sex. Conversely, there's virtually no correct way to play golf.

Unfortunately sex, like golf, has become complicated. Back in the good old days sex was a social activity, and people could engage in it at will. People even played golf and had sex at the same time. It was a wonderful world. But times have changed, and danger lurks behind every seductive smile. You need to choose your sex partners with all the prejudice and discernment that you would a partner for the club invitational. Still, when compared to the horrific evils of golf, sex is far and away the better of the two. Remember, you can always have safe sex, but it's impossible to have safe golf.

CHAPTER
4

Make a searching and fearless moral inventory of yourself.

In golf you're not defined by who you are and what you stand for—people could care less. You're defined by your handicap—the one number that informs the shallow, petty world of golf of everything anybody needs to know about you. Work with AIDS patients, provide shelter for the homeless, or establish an endowment fund that will guarantee that every underprivileged child in your home state can attend college—big deal. If you're a 20, you're a 20, and you still suck.

There are qualifications to this standard. Such as whether you are a good 20 or a bad 20. On the odd chance that we pull your name from a blind draw, we need to know whether or not you are a good, or reliable, 20. Are you, on any given day, going to go out and shoot between 94 and 98? If yes, then you are a good 20. We know what you are and we can deal with you.

On the other hand, if you're a 20 because half of your scores are 94 to 98, and the other half feature triple digits and a sob story on why you didn't break 100, you are a bad 20. Bad 20s are of no use to anyone. If you are going to post something in the mid-nineties on a regular basis, a partner of superior playing ability, which in your case could be just about anybody, can work with you in a match. If it's a toss-up as to whether you're going to shoot 93 or 123, it would be best if you went away.

Many golfers who fall into the second category will hold up the USGA handicap system as defense. "I shouldn't be a twenty, I should be a twenty-eight," they'll cry. "If they used all my scores my average would be around a hundred, therefore I should get twenty-eight shots," they'll add, commenting on the USGA's process of using only the lower half of all scores posted to figure handicaps. There is nothing more pathetic than a grown man pleading for mercy while simultaneously begging people to lower his already shallow opinion of them.

The USGA handicap system is terribly flawed. It rewards consistency and punishes those with random scoring habits. But whining on and on about it bores everyone within earshot. There's nothing worse than a problem golfer complaining about the injustices of the country's standardized system of measuring golf potential. That's right—potential. This may be news to you, but the arcane USGA handicap system wasn't created to average out your scores. Your dog could average out your scores.

According to the USGA, the handicap system was developed *to make the game of golf more enjoyable by enabling golfers of differing abilities to compete on an equitable basis.* Yeah, right. If that's the case then why do they *disregard high scores that bear little relation to the player's potential scoring ability.* Playing opponents don't disregard scores that bear little relation to our potential scoring ability. They laugh their asses off at our scores that bear little relation to our potential: "Nice snowman. You lose the hole and the press. Pay me at the bar."

Feeling betrayed, we courageously, albeit defensively, respond, "But the USGA doesn't recognize that quadruple-bogey eight as my score. The most the USGA will recognize on that hole is six. Since you also made six, it stands to reason, in the eyes of the USGA, that we actually halved the hole. Given that the USGA is the governing body of this great game, how can you possibly overrule them? It looks like a push to me."

"Give me my money, you twerp."

So the USGA handicap system is all about cataloging scores and calculating potential. Ancillary issues like skins, Nassau's, silly-ass games, and presses be damned. For underachievers this is a real nightmare, and when it comes to golf, everyone is an underachiever. It means you're being measured against what you can do, not by what you more than likely will do. Potential is like the jar of peanut butter on the top pantry self. Everybody has some, but few can reach it. For those that do reach it, the USGA has a special gift. They lower your handicap and redefine your potential. In doing so they simultaneously begin to empty your wallet.

This vicious circle is compounded by the odd relationship between what it takes to lower and what it takes to raise a handicap. Though the actual mathematical equation for the USGA index calculation is more closely guarded than the secret formula for Coca-Cola, it goes something like this: It takes one sub-index score to lower a handicap, twenty-eight above-index scores to raise a handicap. This anomaly creates a system ripe for corruption.

By his nature the problem golfer strives to excel at golf. He wants to be considered a player by his peers, a guy who can really golf the ball. He goes to great lengths in order to establish this reputation. Books, videos, magazines, lessons, training aids, sports psychology, and equipment; all purchased in the pursuit of excellence. He'll get up early and go to the driving range before work. He'll skip lunch to practice putting, and leave early to hit a few balls before teeing off in his league. On the weekends he'll play at least twice. After each round he can be found chipping and hitting bunker shots.

He's been to a variety of golf academies, each with a different syllabus. One school for the power game, another for putting, and perhaps a couple to work on his irons. At least three different sports psychologists have been consulted, and he's no stranger to hypnotherapy. He can recite Hogan's Five Lessons, and at the drop of a golf cap he'll compare and contrast the swing philosophies of Jim McLean and David Leadbetter. He has a library of videotape on his own swing that he analyzes ad nauseam. The problem golfer has the focus and persistence of a three-year-old who wants her ragged and tattered blanket.

Everything he does is in one way or another is meant to improve his game. When driving in the car he'll squeeze a rubber ball to strengthen his grip. At work he can be seen twisting his torso, and stretching his arms and shoulders to maintain flexibility. When playing video golf, he will try to hit shots that mirror his own so he can practice visualization and realistic course management. The problem golfer is obsessed with the relentless pursuit of golf perfection.

Given this singular focus, it's likely that the problem

golfer will show short-term improvement. Along the way he will have beaten foes that formerly got the better of him. He may do well, possibly even take home some hardware, and move up a flight or two in the club championship. He'll garner invitations from friends to play in other tournaments. He'll be a hot commodity in scramble events. The problem golfer will begin to experience a sense of accomplishment as he reaps the fruits of his labor. He will have confidence, and he will exude this confidence. He will begin to receive compliments from other golfers and humbly accept them. He will be at one with himself and at peace with the world. His handicap will drop.

There's an old proverb, reported in some circles as being Chinese, which goes like this: Be careful what you wish for, because it may come true. Once he has lowered his handicap to a level where others consider him to be a good golfer, the problem golfer faces the ultimate horror: His USGA designated potential will sink to a level that he can never consistently achieve. He's screwed.

The world revolves around the "net" result. Corporations look for net profits, families have net take-home pay, and golfers—99.9 percent of them anyway—focus on net scores. The problem is this, they're not getting enough shots versus truly excellent players, and they're giving away too many shots to everyone else. They can't beat anybody. They've become too good for their own good.

Here's the problem golfer, strutting around like the cock of the walk, and he can't take two bucks off of the club's sous-chef. He's lowered his handicap to a point that is beyond his grasp. His potential has exceeded his reach. He's splitting fairways, hitting greens, and dropping putts, yet he's dipping into his pocket more often than the father of triplets at an amusement park. This isn't the way it's supposed to be. The problem golfer finds himself on the verge of a breakdown.

Everything he's worked for, everything that he thought was right and just in the universe, has just been proven wrong. He's Al Gore trying to win in Florida, David Caruso once he left *NYPD Blue,* Ian Baker-Finch after winning the British Open. Dazed and confused, the problem golfer is in a state of paranoia. All those that were for him are now against him. What was once right is wrong. He's confusing six-irons with nine-irons, playing in front of the tee markers, failing to abide by the ninety-degree cart-path rule during wet weather. The problem golfer is as baffled as a first-term freshman at a major university. Then the solution hits him: Don't enter any more low scores.

My God, an epiphany. It makes perfect sense in a radical, 1960s sort of way. If this is the way the system operates, he'll manipulate the system to his advantage. If the system is going to punish him for his diligence and perseverance, then the system can reward him for digression, for sliding back a little. But he won't be sliding at all. The problem golfer will be working as hard as ever, playing as well as he ever has. It's just that errors will begin to occur during the transmission of data. This situation calls for a little garbage in, garbage out.

The problem golfer, who never expected that pasting a brand-new index card to his bag-tag would cause so much financial and mental agony, seeks retribution through the only means at his disposal: He cheats. Not the pedestrian brands of cheating—kicking a ball out from under a tree, tapping down a spike mark, failing to mention a lost ball, or taking an illegal drop. This is more of a white-collar fraud: failing to post a sub-index score, or not making that scorecard adjustment, letting that 6 on the par three stay a 6 for recording purposes. Initially the problem golfer believes this is logical and justifiable. As Shakespeare said in *Henry IV*, "For nothing can seem foul to those that win." This is the same thought process the Nixon White House employed when they decided to bug Watergate.

To the problem golfer this is a victimless crime. A little tweak here, a number massage there, and he maintains his high level of play and a manageable handicap. He gets off free and easy. As in other matters of life, the righteous ones pay the toll and suffer for the crimes of others.

We've looked at an opponent's updated handicap card and searched in vain for the 77 he shot while taking us three ways a few weeks earlier, only to spot nothing but eighty-somethings. "Where is it?" we inquire. "I turned it in, there must be a mistake. I'm sure it will pop up the next time," he hastily comments, without eye contact, as he shuffles through his golf bag looking for a conscience. No, it's not a mistake. It's that you're a self-absorbed, spineless weasel, who needs to become the mating interest of a nine-hundred-pound gorilla named Nunchuck.

We all know this type of person. For instance, there's this guy, we'll call him Geoff, but he's known by many names, possibly even your name. Geoff is a fairly decent player. In fact Geoff is one of the better players we know. Geoff's handicap, however, isn't that low, perhaps a 9 or 10. This is odd because he broke 80 six out of the last seven times he played. When confronted with his apparent oversight regarding timely and accurate posting of scores, he says one of the following:

- "I never post the scores I shoot away from my home course."

- "I never post a nine-hole score."

- "I never post the scores I shoot when I play with my kids or my wife."

- "I never post the scores I shoot when I'm on vacation."

- "No one at my club posts their low scores, so if I did I'd be at a disadvantage during club tournaments."

Hey, bite me. Just because you belong to a den of thieves doesn't mean everyone else has to be at a decided disadvantage. Again, from the USGA Handicap System Manual:

A basic premise underlies the U.S.G.A. Handicap System, namely that every player will try to make the best score he can at each hole in every round he plays, regardless of where the round is played, and that he will post every acceptable round for peer review.

There you have it, plain and simple, in black and white. Except there's one problem: Too many golfers use the word *acceptable* in the above sentence as a loophole. They act like they're the Leona Helmsley of the links set—posting corrected scores is for the little people. The word *acceptable* should be removed, end of discussion.

Post every score and try to live up to expectations for once in your worthless life.

Fudging handicaps is more of a problem than cheating on taxes. Who cares if someone cheats on taxes? So one less road gets built—big deal. A few farmers don't get paid not to grow something, no skin off our balata. Taxes is a macro issue, handicap is a micro issue. It affects the people involved personally and immediately. There's a winner and a loser, much of it based on the handicap of the participants. The old saying that a match is won or lost based on the negotiation of strokes on the first tee holds a lot of weight.

We're as much in favor of unfair competitive advantages as the next guy when it comes to business, but this is golf—an endeavor established, and maintained, on the basic principal of honesty and equity among those who partake. By failing to post low rounds the golfers in question become dirty, rotten, stinking cheaters.

About this point you're probably asking, "What does all of this nonsense about handicaps have to do with making a fearless moral inventory in order to quit golf?" Fair question, and one we would expect from a problem golfer. What it has to do is this—you're living a lie. You need to look in the mirror and ask yourself what you're all about, who you are and what you stand for. Just because no one else cares, and rightfully so, this is about you, not everyone else.

It's about taking a long and serious introspective look, and analyzing what you come up with. Don't kid yourself that purchasing Girl Scout cookies and dropping spare change into the Salvation Army kettle at Christmas cleanses your soul and balances your ledger. Symbolic gestures don't mean squat in the big picture. Your big picture currently has all of the appeal of *Caddyshack II.*

Admit it: You don't post all of your scores, and if you do, you certainly don't make the proper adjustments. You probably don't even know you're supposed to make adjustments. Stupidity is not a defense when we're talking about leveling the playing field. We see no circumstances under which you can continue to walk this earth without coming to grips with the fact that you should have an index of at least one or two strokes less than what you currently claim.

Look on the bright side, this reduction will undoubtedly provide you with a short-term boost in admiration from fellow golfers. It will be, of course, offset by a long-term reduction in winnings at the very hands of those showering you with praise for lowering your handicap. We couldn't be more pleased.

Upstanding members of a society don't play hide-and-seek with the truth. In their quest for a lower handicap and higher praise, they more than likely are very diligent in reporting scores. Eager to see their index number drop on the handicap sheets posted in the men's locker room, they skip with glee directly to the pro shop to enter a number that will help deliver them to their golfing Xanadu.

Since we've already concluded that your personal constitution is equivalent to that of the thirty-seventh President of the United States, we surmise your commitment to the truth is on par with his. From Nixon's acceptance speech for the presidential nomination in 1968: "Let us begin by committing ourselves to the truth—to see it like it is, and tell it like it is—to find the truth, to speak the truth, and to live the truth." Eerie how your two paths have paralleled, isn't it?

Now you are here, listlessly hanging in limbo, suffering in golf purgatory. Getting only a stroke or two from guys who used to have you finished by the twelfth hole. Passing out shots by the gross to hacks that at one time used to be in your flight, and you're losing to both groups. The promised land of hard work and perseverance was to be your home. What you once felt would be heaven on earth you're finding to be a living hell. You have stumbled upon the golfer's conundrum: Do you want to play consistently good golf, or do you want to win matches?

You scream, "Both—I want both, damn it. I've earned both, and I bloody well demand both."

You can't have both.

Though they sound synonymous, the two are polar opposites. As a problem golfer you know that having one without the other is like hitting eighteen greens, but finding there is no hole to putt to. What good is it? You want to shoot low scores and win matches, but you can't. Why? Because as good as you have become, you still suck. You are a problem golfer, not a professional golfer. You may be better than anyone you know, but there are still thousands of golfers better than you. You may think you're a big fish, but you're swimming in a small pond loaded with little white balls, and in that body of water they pass out shots on the first tee.

So what are you going to do now that you've been found out? Forget to enter low rounds into the handicap system? We don't think so. Fail to adjust that 81 to a 78, reflecting the quad you took on the easy par five? We tend to doubt it. What you're going to do is conduct a fearless, thorough, and painstakingly precise moral inventory of yourself. Given the problem golfer's oblique nature, your biggest challenge will be to sift through the lies and misinformation that you'll be handing over to yourself. But because you, and all problem golfers, are so one-dimensional, and a thin dimension to boot, there isn't a lot of material to work with. You should finish this project before the replay of *Golf Central*.

Once you've completed this moral inventory and cleaned your house of all of these misdeeds, you will once again be able to stand in judgment by your peers. Taking into account the changes you've implemented and the progress you've made, they will render an opinion. Of course, since you're still a golfer, their opinion doesn't matter. You'll still be defined by your handicap, which basically means you still suck. But it will be a more accurate representation of how much you suck. It would just be easier to quit the game. Then you wouldn't have a handicap and could be judged by other things, such as who you are and what you stand for.

CHAPTER
5

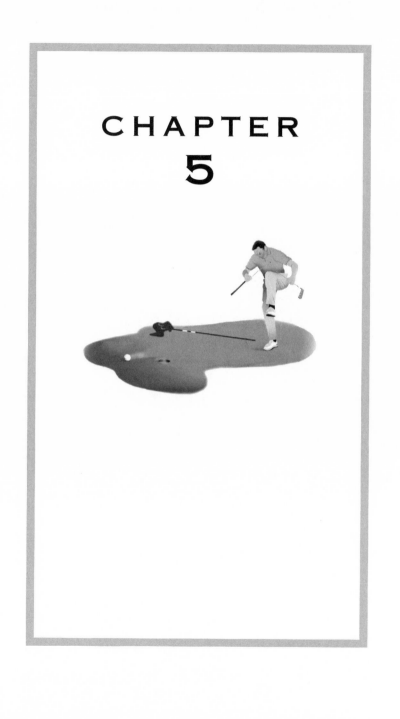

Admit to God, to yourself, and to anyone else who'll listen, the exact nature of your wrongs.

Virtually everything you do on the golf course is wrong. If it weren't, par would be 93. It's not, so it must be you. Your grip is wrong, your setup is wrong, your swing is wrong, your ball flight is wrong, your thinking is wrong, your handicap is wrong (as we established in the previous chapter), and of course, your score is wrong.

It's time to come to terms with the fact that you're a mess. You're also going to have to let God in on the deal, though he probably already knows, and fess up to each and every sorry son of a bitch who happens to end up in the seat next to you. It'll work like this. You sit down next to someone and say, "Hi, I'm so and so. I'm a problem golfer, and I'm about to tell you all about it."

More than likely he'll remove himself without incident. If he stays, he too may have a problem. It may or may not be golf, but if he's interested in listening to what you have to say, he's definitely got some unresolved issues that you're going to hear about. As tedious as this sounds, this is what you want. The theory being that the more often you tell someone what a hopeless embarrassment you've become, the better the chance that you will finally do something to change that.

In order to prove how wrong most everything you do on a golf course is, we will provide a wide range of examples illustrating our point. Our point being, for those unable to fight through subtext, that if you made as many mistakes in other parts of your life as you do in golf, you'd be living in a cardboard box on a heating grate with a three-legged cat, a wardrobe stolen from the Salvation Army, a penchant for generic alcohol, a collection of crusty *Gallery* and *High Society* magazines, a dozen imaginary friends named after U.S. Presidents, a colander, and a tuning fork. The last two items rigged to receive signals from the mother ship.

Most golfing miscues are self-inflicted. The game, however, isn't entirely blameless. Golf invites, cajoles, and double dares us to be risk takers. One of the basic tenets of golf course architecture is the concept of risk and reward. In his book *Golf Course Architecture,* Dr. Michael J. Hurdzan, one of the leading authorities on the subject, and a renown designer in his own right, states, "The architectural spirit of St. Andrews is that golf is a game matching skill and strength to strategy. At St. Andrews, there is no one correct line to the hole, but multiple lines, with hazards balancing risk and reward." The bastards that design these things have been doing this on purpose from the very start.

A classic example of risk/reward on this side of the pond is the par-fives on the back nine of Augusta National. Two itty-bitty holes with a dab of water in front of them, easily reachable in two for the guys with their

names on their bags, but which have caused more col-
lapses than vertigo. Curtis Strange, Fred Couples, and
David Duval each lost green jackets in the narrow stream
that guards the thirteenth. Seve Ballesteros could have
added to his wardrobe were it not for plopping into the
pond in front of fifteen. Chip Beck chose to lay-up on fifteen when he was within a few shots of the lead on Sunday, eliminating the risk, but also eliminating his chance
to win. He was vilified for it. No matter what anyone
says, in this country we cherish car wrecks, and Beck
took away a chance for us to see one. Shame on him.

Golf is like a sting operation, setting you up at every
turn. It's like your best buddies getting you liquored up
and dragging you out to a strip club. Just as the hottest
number in the joint is about to give you a lap dance, your
wife shows up. Out of the corner of the eye your wife
didn't punch, you see your buddies high-fiving, and laughing until beer shoots out of their noses.

As hopelessly difficult as golf courses can be, ultimately you pull the trigger, not the guy who designed the
joint. The architects just sit around high-fiving themselves, and laughing until beer comes out of their noses.
It's not just the outcome of your shots that's of concern.
It goes without saying that you couldn't hit a barn if you
were inside one. The problem is that you probably would
choose to try to hit a ball in one barn door and out the
other.

Statistically speaking, you've got a better chance of
becoming Miss Congo than you do pulling off most of the
shots you try. Not that a three-wood off a shaggy downhill lie, to a front pin on an island green, can't get close
to the flagstick. It's just that the likelihood that you, or any
other human being, will ever do it is remote. It is this type

of shot, or the decision-making behind this type of shot, that is the exact nature of your wrongs.

The Jezebel of poor shot selection is the par five. To begin with, the par five offers more shot decisions to screw up, 25 percent more than a par four, and a whooping 67 percent more than a par three. There's also more landmass to navigate with a par five, usually more hazards, and a high probability that a long iron will be pulled from the bag. All of this creates a scrumptious recipe for disaster.

For example, the fourteenth hole of the Old Course at St. Andrews, a 523-yard par five, has four distinctly different paths to the green. This is serious overkill. Golfers can barely decide which shirt to wear, let alone make a conscious decision on which path to take on any given hole. Most will just hit, and wherever the ball ends up will dictate the path they'll take.

As soon as the problem golfer arrives at the tee of a par five he does something wrong: he starts to think. The thing he thinks about most is "getting home in two." Though this is decidedly foolish, it's not without cause. The problem golfer is saddled with the burden of having an unquenchable thirst for imitating people. This can be especially annoying when the previous evening was spent watching Adam Sandler movies, but equally disturbing when the problem golfer tries to duplicate things that other golfers do. Specifically, the things golfers on TV do.

The reason some golfers are on TV is that they are good enough to be on TV. If they're good enough to be on TV, they're good enough to reach par fives in two. Conversely, if you're not on TV, this should be enough of a clue to figure out that you're not good enough to reach par fives in two. But stopping you would ruin it for the rest of us, so please keep trying.

When it comes to stupid shots on par fives, number one with a bullet is the driver off the fairway. Before the cold-topped orb comes to rest a mere thirty-five yards from its starting point, the problem golfer, with a genuine tone of bewilderment, utters something along the lines of "But I saw Tiger do it." Who cares if you saw Winnie the Pooh and Tigger do it? What in God's name made you, who can barely hit a ball off a tee with an iron, think you could do it?

In the problem golfer's book, however, reaching a par five in two is what it's all about. Why even bother to make a tee-time if you can't rip a few drivers in an effort to give yourself that elusive putt for an eagle. Ah yes, the eagle putt. The siren song of golf. Enticing you to shun peril and abandon all rational thought. Seducing you to hit a shot you've never even attempted, all for the glory of the eagle.

Those of you who stayed awake during Western lit class undoubtedly recall Homer's *Odyssey*—the epic Greek poem, not a putter belonging to the patriarch of an animated TV series. A portion of this tedious tome deals with the main man, Odysseus, being wooed by the song of sirens. The sirens supposedly were these hot, horny babes, singing out with wanton lust for the Greek warriors sailing home from the Trojan War. But the noise could just as easily have been the wind.

Odysseus, bound and determined to get home to his wife Penelope after being away doing guy stuff for more than ten years, needed to have his ears stuffed, eyes blindfolded, and body strapped to the ship's mast in order to resist the temptation of these songs. He must have instinctively known that many weaker men before him had sought refuge, or a little nookie, with these sirens, only to end up shredded, bloodied, and dead along the rocks.

Do you think Odysseus is going to pull out a driver from 238 yards off a tight lie to reach a par five in two? Or do you think Odysseus is going to lay-up to a yardage he feels comfortable with and try to knock a sand wedge tight, giving himself a short putt for birdie? We vote lay-up, but then again, we aced Western lit.

The eagle, however, is just too tempting for problem golfers, the population of which is void of anyone with even a quarter of the mental strength of Odysseus. They will fire over anything on land or sea to reach the Promised Land, and afford them a putt for an eagle. It represents everything they live for: shot execution, lower scores, achievement, notoriety from peers, and, primarily, a story to tell. An eagle has the half-life of a nuclear fuel cell.

A golfer is nothing without his stories, even more so than fishermen. A guy catches a big fish, big deal. It happens all of the time. Who really cares if some weathered old salt spent half a lifetime tracking down, and finally catching, something to hang on his wall? There's no romance in that. If you wanted a fish that badly, they've got loads of them at the grocery store. But you can't buy birdies and eagles, and an eagle, though only one stroke less than a birdie, is a hundred times more valuable during episodes of braggadocio. An eagle story can top any birdie story ever told.

Let's say you run into Johnny Miller sitting at a table rattling off all the birdies he made en route to shooting 63 in the final round to win the 1973 U.S. Open. Granted, a pretty good story, but you can just interrupt and say,

"On a 310-yard par four, I dropped one in on the fly from 137 yards in my league the other day for a deuce." Shuts him right up.

If you've got an eagle to lay on top of any number of birdies, you win. What's yet another ball sinking to a watery grave in a lifetime of sunken dreams, when there's a chance, though improbable, that an eagle could be had, and a story could be told, and told, and told, and told, and told?

The other perplexing thing about going for a par five in two is that the decision process never includes what the probability is that the putt will be made. This follows three lines of reasoning. First, the problem golfer doesn't believe he's going to get there, so why worry about the putt? Second, on the rare occasion that the problem golfer has reached in two, he's missed the putt (more than likely three-putting for par), and figures this time will be no different. Last, given that he's spent a great deal of time in a self-congratulatory, delusional state, he assumes that if he does reach the green, the putt, no matter the distance, is a gimme.

So problem golfers go after every par five they can get their hands on, secure in the belief they will make the putt if they reach the green. This type of self-confidence is worthy of a standing ovation. Unfortunately, it is totally unwarranted praise, because more than 98 percent of the time the ensuing shot after trying to reach a par five in two doesn't take place on the green.

Pissed that they didn't get home in two, and determined to at least make a birdie on a hole where they had mentally penciled in a 3, a problem golfer will try just about anything to get it close. The resulting shot is as comical in its desperation as trying to get a date for New

Year's Eve on the morning of December 31. A myriad of different shots could be left after failing to reach the green in two, but there are a couple that please us to no end.

To begin with, for pure drama and excitement, there's nothing that can beat the long bunker shot. It makes *Rocky I* look like *Rocky and Bullwinkle*. The reason is twofold. First, if there's one given in life it's that when a tour player on TV has a long bunker shot, an announcer will state that it is the toughest shot in golf. We've heard it so often it's ingrained in our mind like the Pledge of Allegiance. So now when any golfer gets in the sand for a shot between twenty-five and fifty yards, he immediately thinks of someone like Vern Lundquist spouting on about how the long bunker shot is the hardest in golf.

Second, it is the hardest shot in golf. How cool is this? There's the problem golfer, having all but chiseled an eagle on his scorecard while back on the tee, hitting three from a bunker the architect put in for framing purposes. (Side note for those who are reading this for giggles and grins, but have no intention of quitting the game: Hitting into a framing bunker is terrible. If you ever do land in a framing bunker, you should quit the game.)

With the eagle having realistically flown the coop, and a lifetime of brainwashing about how the difficulty factor of the long bunker shot is equivalent to that of an upside-down, triple salchow, the problem golfer contemplates how to get it close. Get it close? It's not even going to get on the green. Everyone in the foursome knows it, including the guy attempting to get out of the bunker, which is the main reason he's not going to get it out of the bunker (but that's someone else's book).

What happens next is pure vaudeville. Before anything, before he gets out of the cart, looks at his lie, checks the wind, chooses a club, steps into the sand, takes his stance, and adjusts his crotch, the problem golfer announces with resolve, and loud enough for the rest of the foursome to hear, "Ya know, this is the hardest shot in golf." Yes, we know. Now hurry up. The sooner you hit, the sooner you'll be able to try and hit that shot again from virtually the same place.

Armed with something absolutely ill suited for the project at hand, perhaps a seven-iron, maybe a nine-wood, the problem golfer slogs into the bunker, grinds in his heels to form a stance (which is wrong, but again, someone else's book), and flails. After this there are three things certain to happen. One, more sand will be moved than T. E. Lawrence rode across as he led the Arab revolt against the Turks in World War I. Two, his playing partners will be asked where the ball went. Three, there will be loud swearing. All of which is great folly for the other players in the group.

If the driver off the deck somehow manages to avoid a bunker, any of the other shots, most from distances best described as "in between," will create excellent theater. Our personal favorite is the flop wedge off hardpan. If you're looking for proof that the devil keeps a condo at a residential golf development somewhere on earth, this shot should be sufficient confirmation. It is impossible to cleanly slide a sixty-degree wedge under a ball 1.68 inches in diameter that is sitting on tarmac.

The reason the flop shot off hardpan is such a gas is that it carries with it the chance that the person attempting the shot will injure, or perhaps even kill, another problem golfer. Having mentioned this, we want to reiterate that even though our goal is to reduce the number of problem golfers, we intend to do it through guidance and this step-by-step process, not through slaughter. But if one or two problem golfers accidentally get taken out, so be it.

Launched with bazooka-like force as the leading edge of the wedge catches the middle of the ball, this shot will travel a greater distance than a ball hit with a driver from the fairway. Intellectually it would make more sense to blade a wedge from the fairway as opposed to hitting a driver, but now we're sliding into the uncharted waters of golfing logic, and we'd prefer not to go there.

The flop shot off hardpan makes about as much sense as giving a six-year-old a handgun and a fifth of whiskey. But it will be attempted, and the reason it will be tried is the same reason problem golfers do everything: They saw it on TV. They saw someone hit a driver off the fairway on TV so they tried it. The four-wood bump and run was first seen on TV, so they tried it. Everything problem golfers try, they first saw on TV, but none of it works. And you thought TV was just bad for kids.

As a nation, we should forget about blocking objectionable material from children's eyes for the moment, and focus in on an issue of national importance. Who cares if children see more people stop a bullet in the skull, lose a limb, or get vaporized by some future-tech villain? So what if children surfing through cable channels late at night stumble upon the Playboy Channel? For the safety and sanctity of golfers everywhere, the V-chip should be used to scramble TV coverage every time a tour pro attempts to hit anything but a run-of-the-mill shot. If someone loads-up an iron from more than 230 yards, the screen goes blank. If a guy's going to try to splice a three-wood through a thicket of trees, go to a commercial. If John Daly does anything, switch to *Heidi*.

With golf-shot mimicry booming out of control, we need to offer some perspective on how much better the guys on TV are than you. Let's say that you take lessons from a PGA club professional, not that anything you do on the course reflects that, but this is hypothetical, so play along. The pro is probably a decent golfer, and obviously everything he does, he does way better than you. He may also play in state tournaments. Perhaps he may have even won a couple of these events. For purposes of comparison we'll figure the distance between your golfing skills and his skills is approximately the distance between New York City and Boston.

Now look at the difference between your PGA club professional and almost any run-of-the-mill PGA Tour player. Considering everything involved, we would say the approximate disparity in playing ability between your PGA club professional and a PGA Tour player is the distance from New York City to Europa, one of Jupiter's moons, give or take a little. Tiger Woods, by the way, is on Alpha Centauri.

In other words, the PGA club professional has a much better chance of dropping to your level of miserable play than he has of ascending to that of a Tour player. This is one of the reasons most PGA club professionals appear to be one playing lesson away from a nervous breakdown.

There you are on a Saturday morning, standing on the practice range with your dedicated, knowledgeable, and patient PGA club professional. You're trying to learn how to hit a nine-iron. Nothing seems to be working and he wants to illustrate what he is trying to get you to do. So he hits a nine-iron. It starts off low, climbs quickly, and lands softly. It's perfect. You then spend the next forty-five minutes trying to replicate the shot your instructor just hit. You never come close. You go home dejected; he goes back to the area of the clubhouse where all sharp objects have been removed.

That afternoon while lying on your couch, in between sipping beer and dozing off, you watch golf on TV. For example, lets say it's the 2000 Canadian Open, and you've woken up just in time to see Tiger Woods play the final hole. His drive goes into the bunker on the right side of the fairway. He's about 218 yards away, over a pond, to a back right pin position on a narrow green. He hits a six-iron to twelve feet, gets up and down for birdie, and wins the tournament.

The next morning, during your Sunday round, you find yourself in a fairway bunker on hole where the green is fronted by a pond. You pull out a mid-iron and go for it, even though the only thing you've proven is that forty-five minutes is not enough time for you to learn how to hit a nine-iron. Nevertheless, you think you can hit a six-iron out of a fairway bunker, over water, and onto the green, though you've never even imagined hitting a shot like that, let alone practiced it—you've just seen the greatest golfer in the universe do it on TV, so you figured it must not be that difficult. Do yourself a favor: Throw a putter through your TV screen.

We are a nation of excuse mongers, so tossing out a defense such as trying to emulate Tour pros is not unexpected. But no one can go on living like this. These pros that we're so enamored of may make one, possibly two, poor shot decisions per tournament. Problem golfers make that many on the practice green. At some point you have to realize that this isn't working.

We read somewhere that the definition of insanity is

doing the same thing over and over again, and doing it wrong each time. Do we have a winner? How long have you been trying to get rid of that slice? Forever? Those putting yips? Since you picked up the game? Let us reiterate the painful truth that handicaps haven't gone anywhere in twenty years. One of the reasons golfers don't improve is that they keep doing the same things wrong every time they set foot on closely mown grass. Another reason is that they're golfers, and there's so little to work with.

Old-school thinking would suggest that if you stopped making the same mistakes day in and day out your game would get better. No kidding. But they call it the old school for a reason: It's washed up, antiquated thinking. That school bell rusted along time ago. The new-school thinking is this: Pavlov's dogs were smarter than you. When they didn't get the response they were looking for, they quit.

The act of engaging a friend or stranger in confessional conversation regarding your wrongdoings is not an easy one. Without question you will meet some resistance. People may ignore you, shy away, fall asleep, or report you to building security. Rest assured, eventually you will come across someone willing to lend an ear and offer support. There are more than six million problem golfers out there. Each of them playing the game and feeling miserable about it. It won't take long for you to find a kindred spirit, a fellow problem golfer; a person who will empathize with your droning on about poor shot selection, and commiserate with you about your disastrous results.

Tell them about the ball washers you've hit with heeled tee-balls; how you started calling your three kids by the names of the other people in your foursome; the forty-seven sick days you took last year though you haven't had anything worse than a sniffle since grade school; the imitation Masters jacket you wear while pretending that you're hosting the past champions dinner. Tell as many people as you can—they'll be happy you did.

But for now let's keep it to people. Even though the fifth step of *How to Quit Golf* is to *admit to God, to yourself, and to anyone else who'll listen, the exact nature of your wrongs,* we're beginning to think you may want to leave God out of this discussion for a while. No matter how close to God you may feel you are, we believe man only gets so much conference time. Perhaps a conversation with him regarding how you saw Phil Mickelson hit a flop shot over his head and onto the green, and then you tried it, and in doing so effectively neutered the fourteen-year-old boy who was caddying for you, won't be a long-term positive, if you know what we mean.

CHAPTER
6

*You've become entirely ready to have God
remove all these defects of character.*

Problem golfers function under a modified Cartesian philosophy of "I golf, therefore I am." Which is not to say they argue the existence of golf, but quite conversely, that they exist because of golf. Golf is their epicenter, their gyroscope. Everything in their lives plays second fiddle to golf. Given a choice between golf and anything else, there is nothing else—there's only golf.

Golf is the problem, but the things problem golfers do because of golf are by-products of their obsession. By removing golf, you also remove their boorish behavior and inane idiosyncrasies. The problem golfer will, on the outside at least, begin to exhibit the appearance of a normal, socially aware human being. Someday she may even have the potential to offer something positive to society. We're not asking for biblical-type miracles, we're just trying to get people to quit golf, which is enough to ask out of one book.

From the problem golfer's perspective, what he does, and how he does it, is as natural as waking up in the morning. From the cannibal's point of view, noshing on a plump, slow-roasted femur seems entirely reasonable, but that type of behavior is discouraged among the general populace—as are the actions of problem golfers. To illuminate these errors, we are going to take an inside look at the life of a problem golfer, the inappropriately named Bobby Jones.

In this chapter we'll examine a typical week. In Chapters Nine and Twelve we'll continue to follow him as he comes to grips with his golfing addiction, and the steps he takes to bring his life in order. As Voltaire said: "It is not love that should be depicted as blind, but self-love."

A WEEK IN THE LIFE

Monday

It's been less than twenty-four hours, and the sting of defeat is still biting at Bobby Jones as he rides up to his office on the twelfth floor. No way, no way did he and his partner lose to those two gomers, he thinks to himself. Just as the elevator door opens, he shouts out, "No friggin' way," and John Cavanaugh, senior vice president for international sales, barrels out of the elevator entrance.

As the doors close, Jones quickly decides that he has no interest in international advertising. No decent golf courses, if any courses at all, in those fourth-world countries in which Cavanaugh's trying to develop market share. Besides, international advertising isn't a career path, but a sentence. How anybody gets clients these days without throwing a mountain of golf, and the requisite balls, shirts, and hats, at every person with even the slightest say in the decision is beyond him. And how in world did he ever lose a match to Tantillo and Zydeck?

Coffee in hand, Jones opens his bottom, left-hand desk drawer, grabs a couple of Hostess Cupcakes, and begins to listen to the harangue of voice mails collected from noon Friday till now. He shuffles through his day planner, reworking his entire schedule for the week, and logs on to his e-mail. "Nice drive, Jones," spouts Zydeck's high-pitched, adolescent-like voice through the speakerphone. "Don't you hate losing the match on the last hole like that? You can take some pride, however, in being the first person to clear Mrs. Scaramouche's three-story Tudor. Breaking the windshield of her brand-new Mercedes was a stroke of bad luck. Stroke and distance actually. See you Sunday for the rematch. Have a nice day." Bastard.

The obligatory e-mail from Tantillo had been posted. It read, "You suck," in Chiller font, 72-point type, in vibrant magenta letters. Jones was somewhat impressed by this bold, yet minimalist approach, and made a note to search for the most obtrusive, annoying typeface for his return volley next Monday after he surely avenged this most humiliating defeat.

Back to the day planner. All lunches this week have to be scrapped; this time needs to be devoted to keeping his tee-ball off of Mrs. Scaramouche's property. But Thursday could be a problem. The last ad campaign didn't work out well and the Daisy Girl Deodorant account is beginning to show signs of falling apart. To make matters worse, the marketing guys aren't golfers. "Damn it," Jones accidentally blurts out. "I made a pact with myself never to do business with non-golfers—it muddies up the works."

"Do you need anything?" asks Bernice, Jones's secretary, as she sticks her head in his office door.

"No. Wait, yes. Call the Daisy Girl Deodorant boys and see if we can switch the venue for Thursday's meeting. Tell them to meet me at my club," Jones says.

"They don't golf."

"Tell them that I've reserved one of the private dining rooms for our meeting."

"Let me rephrase this. They don't golf, you mindless fool," says Bernice.

"There are two types of people in this world, Bernice. Those who play golf, and those who are about to play golf. The Daisy Girl Deodorant boys are the latter—they just don't know it yet."

"Remember the last time you tried to force-feed golf on unwilling participants. Mr. Dotage sent you to Alaska to try and get the Halibut on a Stick account," Bernice reminds him.

"I would have won that business too if it wasn't for the nitwits in the media department. Besides, that was a long time ago, Bernice. I've forgotten it, I'm sure Dotage has forgotten it, and I suggest you forget it."

Tuesday

After stopping off at the course to practice putting, Jones enters his office ninety minutes late, with his putter shoved up his shirtsleeve to his armpit. He tells Bernice he has a conference call to join and to take a message if anyone phones. Jones immediately shuts the door and pulls out a Putt Accelerator putting mat.

The work he did on the green this morning did nothing to correct—in fact it may have exacerbated—the slight push he'd been experiencing on left-to-right putts between five and seven feet from the hole. Rolling out the Accelerator, he realizes he hasn't brought any of his golf balls from the car. He looks with disgust at the orange box of Titleist DTs stamped with the company's logo. "I can't practice with these rocks," Jones says out loud to no one in particular, an annoying habit of his. "The feel will be wrong, and practicing with them could do more harm than good. Hacks like Tantillo and Zydeck use these balls. Shameless clients grab these things up like mints at a restaurant." But there's no time to go down to the car and retrieve his Slazenger Balatas. He dumps all twelve of the DTs on the floor.

"Who are you talking to?" Bernice asks as she enters his office, uninvited.

"I didn't say anything. What do you want?" Jones snaps back, kicking the golf balls behind the door.

"Lily called this morning. She says you were supposed to take the kids to school today, and that if you had to leave so early you should have told her last night. She missed her Tae Bo class because of you," Bernice scolds him.

"I'm on this call. Is there anything else?"

"She also wants to remind you that she has a mammogram this afternoon, and that you absolutely, positively have to pick up the kids from school."

"Whatever. Are we done?"

"You might be more convincing if you actually opened a phone line," she says as she slams the door on her way out.

"I'm through listening to you."

For the second time this morning Jones starts to work on his putting. With a Hostess Ho Ho firmly clenched be-

97

tween his teeth, he toes the balls to the five-foot mark on the Accelerator and slowly strokes putt after putt. The bad news is that they're still going slightly to the right. The good news is that it's Tuesday, and the revenge match isn't until Sunday. He swallows the chocolate delight in one gulp and decides to call Brockbank, his partner, and see if he intends to practice.

"Brockbank, I was at the practice green at seven-thirty this morning. What have you been doing to clean up your putting problems?" inquires Jones.

"I have a life," counters Brockbank.

"Screw your life, we have a score to settle," he yaps back.

"Don't worry about me, OK. I'm not the one bouncing his drives off imported luxury sedans. Don't forget that I made nine pars," says Brockbank.

"Great, nine pars and nine Xs. You still didn't make a putt. What'd you shoot, ninety-five, ninety-six?"

"Eighty-six. Listen, I've got to go. My job requires my attention. Unlike you, I can make a difference in people's lives," Brockbank says as he hangs up.

"Doctors—it's always about them, isn't it? I can't believe I have a podiatrist as a partner," Jones says out loud. "They're not even real doctors, are they? What do they do, work on feet? Who the hell wants to spend their entire life looking at feet? Next year a new partner is in order—someone who can putt, and definitely not a doctor."

"Who are you talking to?" Bernice bellows from her desk.

"Don't you have coffee to make?" Jones responds.

Speaking of doctors, Jones remembers he has a lesson this afternoon, and had better call his wife. After searching for her number for a minute or two with no luck, he yells out to Bernice, "I can't find my wife's work number."

"She quit working three years ago, after your third child was born. Try her at home, you moron," she indignantly yells back.

Jones contemplates hiring a new secretary, but they're harder to find than golfing partners who can putt. "Hi, honey, it's me. How important is this mammogram thing?"

It's apparent that the lesson is going to have to be moved.

Wednesday

This morning's short game practice lasted longer than expected. As Jones enters the office around ten-thirty, the rumor mill is rife with talk about the acquisition of a small agency in Great Britain. He quickly fires off an apologetic e-mail to John Cavanaugh regarding his unexplained rant on the elevator Monday morning. There are great golf courses in Scotland and England, and he can think of no finer way to see them than on the corporate tab.

Bernice bursts in, "You have fifteen voice mails from yesterday. You really should stick around after lunch one of these days; it's amazing what you can get done. I wrote down most of them, but there are a few I thought you should hear for yourself."

Jones hits the message button on the phone. Message one: "You still suck."

Message two: "Mr. Jones, this is Matt Norris. I'm a life-long friend of, and an attorney who represents, Mrs.

Gladys Scaramouche. Your Slazenger Balata with the red RTJ scribbled next to the number was found imbedded in the windshield of Mrs. Scaramouche's Mercedes this Sunday past. It's our understanding that your insurance coverage will be sufficient for the damage to the automobile, but they have told us that you have no liability coverage. This is a shame, Mr. Jones, because Baby Snivels, Mrs. Scaramouche's prize schipperke, was in the front seat of her Mercedes when the incident occurred. That Baby Snivels soiled the fine leather in Mrs. Scaramouche's three-week-old Mercedes is regrettable, but that situation has been attended to.

"What doesn't appear to be easily remedied is the uneasiness that has overcome Baby Snivels. As I'm sure you're aware, schipperkes are easily agitated, and Baby Snivels is not an exception to the rule. I'll cut to the chase, Mr. Jones. You scared the crap out of Baby Snivels, resulting in his catatonic state. We are looking for full compensatory damages."

Message three: "Jones, this is Dotage. You might remember the name. I was the guy who hired you. I can also be the guy who fires you. Where were you at breakfast this morning? You know how I hate to eat my porridge alone."

Message four: "You couldn't suck any more if you tried."

Jones lets out a big sigh and reaches for the cupcake drawer. "Screw the dog," he mutters to himself. "Just because the mutt loses control of his bowels in the front seat of the old lady's Benz doesn't mean I caused it to have a nervous breakdown. Dotage is a non-event. The guy could be dead by lunch. Tantillo and Zydeck, however, are becoming pests. They must be silenced."

But Jones feels woefully ill prepared for the rematch.

It's already the middle of the week, and he's in desperate need of more practice time. He calls the Daisy Girl Deodorant boys and feels them out about the idea of a little golf after the lunch meeting. They hate the idea, but Jones is sure they'll come around once they get in the country club atmosphere.

There are thirty minutes to spare before a hastily scheduled meeting with Dotage to review the Daisy Girl Deodorant strategy, if you can call it that. Jones leans back in his chair and stares at the ceiling as he momentarily ponders his place in the world: thirty-seven years old; an increasing waistline and cholesterol count due to a diet centered on food that can be bought at the turn; a wife whose looks, personality, and opinions only vaguely resemble those of the woman he married twelve years ago; two kids with parochial school tuition biting away at money he could be using for golf academies and equipment upgrades; a car that is supposed to convince the neighbors that he's an unqualified success, but is one or two classes more than he can afford; a house that would have cost half as much if he hadn't felt the need to flock to the trendy part of town; an anemic 401(k) plan that will have to be supplemented with lottery winnings if he's to retire before seventy-five; a job in advertising, enough said; a primary client who sells powdery deodorant to teenage girls; a golf game that refuses to show any interest in improvement no matter the effort he gives; and a firm belief that he would give it all up if he could break par just once in his life.

He snaps out of it and realizes that there's enough time to get in some drills. Standing up, he straddles his chair and grips it between his knees. From this position he practices his take-away, rotating his shoulders back behind an imaginary ball. This has become his favorite drill, building resistance in the hips, creating torque, and developing muscle memory for a powerful swing.

"Does your wife Lily know you're having an affair with your chair?" Dotage asks as he enters Jones's office, twenty minutes early.

Thursday

"Forty-five, Barry, I shot a friggin' forty-five in my league last night," Jones howls into his cell phone while noshing on a Twinkie, balancing a cup of coffee between his knees, and negotiating three lanes of morning rush hour traffic. "How bad was it? I'll tell you how bad it was. No greens, Barry, I didn't hit a single friggin' green. I haven't shot forty-five since I was in high school. I've got to see you this morning. No, I've got business this afternoon; it's got to be this morning. You're booked? On a Thursday morning, you're kidding me. Who do you have? Perchard? He needs a whole team of golf professionals to help him out. Morman? A basket case, why bother? He pays you cash, fine. Who else? There must be someone you can cancel. Mrs. Scaramouche? You've got old lady Scaramouche? Cancel the bitch—she's suing me. Claims I gave her dog the runs and now the mutt's on suicide watch. Yes, Baby Snivels. She says I've made him schizophrenic. Hell, I'd be nuts too if I had to listen to her squawk all day long.

"What do you mean you can't bump her? Hell, she's got to be a hundred and fifteen years old. One more golf lesson is going to do as much good as another collagen treatment. You're not banging her, are you, Barry? You're not cozying up to the old lady to make a run at her

money, are you? Here's the deal, Barry—cancel Scaramouche or I move my company's golf outing. I swear it,
Barry, I'll move the whole thing, including the entire shirt
order that I let you mark up three hundred percent. I'm
desperate here, Barry. Good. I'll see you in an hour."

Jones's phone rings before he gets a chance to set it
down. "Lily's been calling every five minutes for an hour,
and Dotage wants you to call," Bernice hollers through
the earpiece.

"Tell my wife I'll get to her when I can. Call Dotage
and tell him I'm on a conference call, and that I'll meet
him for breakfast tomorrow morning. I'm running late for
the Daisy Girl Deodorant boys."

Jones replaces the cell phone in his right hand with
the coffee cup, and grabs for another Twinkie under the
seat with his left. The minor issue of directing the car is
relegated to his knees. The phone hasn't even cooled
from the previous calls when it rings again. Stuffing the
snack cake in his mouth, he gracefully shifts the coffee
from his right to his left hand, grabs the phone with his
right, and changes lanes with his knees. If he could only
create this kind of chemistry on the golf course, he'd be
on the PGA Tour.

"Hello, Mr. Dotage," he says, anticipating a call from
the boss. "Oh, hi honey, what's up? Oh, crap, I forgot,
can't make it tonight. I've got the Daisy Girl Deodorant
boys at the club this afternoon. I know they didn't used to
play golf, but all of a sudden they wanted to give it a try.
What am I supposed to do? Well, I know the counseling
is important, but so is my job. If this Daisy Girl Deodorant account leaves, you and the kids can forget about Disney World this fall," Jones says.

"Trust me, I wouldn't be out here if it weren't absolutely imperative. You know how I hate playing with non-golfers. I'd rather spend the entire day at counseling than deal with this nightmare I'm about to face. But ultimately, you know I'm doing it for you and the kids. OK, gotta run. I might be late, love you."

Jones's lesson goes well, just a minor adjustment at the top of the back swing. He has it going on line, even drawing it at the end. But the idea of getting any serious work done on his game while careening about the course with the Daisy Girl Deodorant boys was seriously flawed. The only thing it accomplishes is to confirm his philosophy of never doing business with non-golfers. Not only are the Daisy Girl Deodorant boys incapable of advancing the ball in the air, they're also predisposed to playing out the entire hole, regardless of the carnage they're leaving in their wake.

The net result for the afternoon looks like this: Number of players: 4. Number who had played more than nine holes in their life: 1. Holes completed: 8.5. Playing time: 3 hours and 48 minutes. Balls used: 53. Balls lost: 51. Groups playing through: 6. Beverage cart service stops: 7. Total beverage cart tab: $228.18. Divots in the fairway: 1. Divots on the green: 5. Total carts utilized: 4. Carts slightly damaged: 2. Carts totaled: 1. Carts submerged in the pond in front of the eighth green: 1. Clubs broken: 5. Clubs lost: 3. Highest score on one hole: 17. Lowest score on one hole: 3 (Jones birdied the first). Total number of strokes tallied by the foursome: 254. Ill will created by taking the Daisy Girl Deodorant boys out on the golf course: immeasurable.

Friday

There was no way Jones was going to make breakfast with Dotage, but he knew that when he promised he'd be there. Whatever flaws produced the Tudor-clearing, windshield-impaling slice appear to be gone, only to have been replaced by a new strain of golfing virus—the snap hook. Jones had to opt out of breakfast in order to fix this problem. Dotage could have someone else mop the drool off his chin this morning. Working on the dumbest account in the history of advertising was draining. He granted himself some comp time, and hit the speed dial number on his cell phone for the pro shop, though it wasn't more than fifty yards from where he stood on the practice tee.

"Hey, Barry, I'm down at the range, wait till you see what I've got going today," Jones says. "Wait a sec, I've got another call. This is Jones. Oh, hi honey, let me call you right back, I'm on with Dotage. No, he canceled breakfast, but let me call you back. All right, Barry, I'm here. Listen, it's going left, really left, you've got to get down here. OK, but try to hustle up, I've got to visit the office at some point this morning."

Jones bangs a few more drives, and is totally lost on how the ball can be going that low, that quickly, and that left, when the phone rings again. "This is Jones. For crying out loud, I just got off the phone, Lily, what's digging at your shorts? No, I don't think I can meet up with you and the kids this afternoon. Brockbank has already called me three times this morning. He wants to get in a quick nine this afternoon before our match Sunday, and I've already committed. I shouldn't be late. I'll call you on my way home. Maybe I'll pick up some pizza, love you, bye."

Jones punches in the number of Brockbank's office and begins to speak. "Hi, it's Mr. Jones, is Dr. Brockbank there? Yes, it's somewhat of an emergency. Of what nature? Well, you could tell Dr. Brockbank if we lose this weekend he's going to wish he were a proctologist because he's going to have a Great Big Bertha up his ass. Does that sound like an emergency to you, sweetheart?

"Brockbank, Jones here. What do you mean? I didn't say anything wrong to her; just tell her to lighten up. Can you clean your schedule for this afternoon? I've freed up my entire day to work on my game, and I think I can make time to help you with your putting. Meet me on the green around two—no, make it two-thirty. If I can convince Barry to give me a playing lesson this morning, that will take me until noon, then I'll run to the office, throw some water on whatever fire my secretary's started, and be back here by two-thirty to straighten you out. I've got to run."

Jones cranks another half dozen balls to the left. "Barry, where the hell are you?" he screams at the pro shop as his cell phone rings once again.

"This is Jones," he yaps into the phone. "Yes, what is it, Bernice, and don't tell me Dotage called. He didn't call. He's right there. Great, put him on. Hello, Mr. Dotage, how are you? Pardon me? Breakfast, oh yes, about breakfast. To be perfectly honest, sir, I think I've created a monster. I had every intention of joining you this morning, sir, but like I was saying. Pardon me, yes, I did promise that I would meet you this morning for breakfast, but as I was saying, I think I've created a monster here, sir.

"You know I had those boys from Daisy Girl Deodorant out on the golf course yesterday. Yes, sir, I know. I didn't think they liked to golf either, sir. But I took them out yesterday, and lo and behold, they loved the game. Just ate it up, sir. And you know what you always say: The client comes first. Right now, as we speak, I'm having my very own personal teaching pro give them a group lesson, and then we're going to go out and play again. Yes, sir, imagine that. I've got to run now, sir, they just called our tee-time. Yes, I suspect that I'll have approval on the new campaign in no time, sir. Yes, sir, a very important account. I agree, sir; body odor isn't something to laugh about. No, sir, we can't have a country filled with stinky teenage girls. That would be a national disaster, sir. Yes, sir, I'm sure every teenage boy in America thinks of us as heroes too, sir. No, sir, I don't think we're contributing to the rise in premarital sex because we help make young women smell as fresh as daisies. Yes, sir, once this is all wrapped up, you and I will definitely get together for breakfast. Wouldn't miss it, sir, and thank you. Could you put my secretary on the line?

"You're a dead woman."

Saturday

Jones wonders when Little League started playing on Saturday mornings. It wasn't that way when he was growing up. Monday and Wednesday were National League, Tuesday and Thursday were American League. Clean and simple, left the weekends for his father to play golf and mow the yard. Kids today, too much stuff going on.

Grabbing his sand wedge and shag bag from the car, Jones heads over to a grassy area that looks like a good place for hitting wedges while waiting for the game.

Jones begins to hit short chip shots off of the artificial turf practice mat he keeps in his trunk. This is perfect, he thinks, he can work on his short game and watch his son play ball at the same time.

A burst of applause startles Jones, and he sees that the ball game had started, and that his son, Cameron, is standing on second base. He wonders how he got there. No problem, he figures, he'll surely tell his dad what happened on the way home. He continues hitting wedges, extending the distance to fifty yards or so. He hits a couple of dozen, chases them down, gathers them up, and hits them back toward the mat. Then a shank. What went wrong there? he asks himself. Another one flares off to the right, and a third. OK, just losing concentration. Now is a good time to watch an inning or two of the game.

He walks over to the fence and tries to find his son, forgetting exactly what position he plays. Shortstop—no, that's his daughter. He gazes over the field, but doesn't see him. Thinking this is odd, he quickly realizes that his son's team, the Tigers, are at bat. The Indians are in the field. He recalls that one of the Daisy Girl Deodorant boys has a son who plays left field for the Indians. What if Cameron hit a ball over the Daisy Girl Deodorant kid's head? he thinks. Now that would be a stupid way to lose an account.

An inning or so goes by. Has baseball always been this boring? Jones figures it's time to see if those shanks have disappeared and picks up his wedge and shag bag and heads back to grassy area. He chips a few, no problem. Hits a dozen to about twenty-five yards, and a dozen more to fifty yards. It looks like the shanks are gone, and he decides to hit a couple of full wedges before packing it in.

He wrists the ball around until he finds a nice tuft of grass, draws his club back, stopping at the top of his back swing, and looks over his right shoulder to see if it's in position. Everything looks A-OK. Back to address, Jones makes a slight forward press, then back, and through. Whack. That doesn't feel good at all. Where'd it go? He looks straight, nothing, then to the right. Another shank. "Oh God," he blurts, as the ball heads directly at the left fielder. "Fore! Fore in left field!" Jones screams. The kid's not moving. Of course he's not moving—who the hell yells fore at a baseball game? "Fore!" Oh no—he realizes it's the Daisy Girl Deodorant kid. "Fore, in left field. Hey, Daisy Girl Deodorant kid, look out, fore!" He never saw it coming.

Sunday

The front nine does not go well. Jones was fighting that hook all morning, and though he managed to keep the ball in bounds, that's about all he's been able to do. The golf course looks entirely different from the left side of each hole. Because he's a life-long fader of the ball, there are bunkers out there he's never seen before.

Brockbank is a waste. If he's going to play like this, he may as well keep Sunday hours. It's painfully obvious to Jones that Brockbank hasn't touched a club since he threw his bag in his trunk last Sunday. Granted, Jones did find the water on number seven, but all Brockbank had to do was two-putt from seven feet to halve the hole. Had he done that, the team would have been down one with two holes to play on the front. Not two down going into number eight.

"Listen, Brockbank," Jones says, "We need to get

going here. Can I tell you something? You're playing like crap, you know that, don't you? You suck right now. You suck a lot. What'd you take on the front, forty-seven, forty-eight? My God, when did you start golfing, this morning?

"I told you a dozen times you needed to get out and practice, didn't I?" Jones continues to badger his partner. "Well, I guess I'm vindicated on that one. Listen, we need to shake these guys up, so I doubled the bet on the back. A hundred dollars for the nine, and a hundred dollars for the total. Yeah, I know that we're four down after nine, I saw you get us there, but the only way I could double the bet on the back was to give them a double on the total. Quit whining, quit sucking, and start playing some golf."

Brockbank makes birdie on the short, par four tenth, so maybe the pep talk worked, but Jones doubts it. He has zero confidence in this guy, figures he's done, and the rest is up to him. The eleventh is a par five, with water all the way down the left. Jones faded the ball his entire life until the round with the Daisy Girl Deodorant boys, so he never worried about this hole, but now it's got him petrified.

Jones starts to pump himself up. "I've played this hole hundreds of times," he says aloud. "Just make five and walk away. I'm not getting home in two, so just put something in the fairway. Don't let Zydeck and Tantillo dictate my game." Biting his lower lip, he grabs a five-iron, and hits it into the left rough off of the tee, no more than six feet from the water. "I can't even lay-up properly," he again says aloud. Brockbank is in the middle of the fairway.

Jones hits a five-iron again for his second, this time aiming way over toward the right rough. It barely stays dry as it rolls to a stop in the left rough, two feet short of the water. "That shot almost boomeranged back to me," says Jones says in disgust. Brockbank hits his second in the short grass. "Will miracles never cease?" Jones says as he pulls out a seven-iron. "I've never hit anything more than a nine-iron into this green, but I'm still dry."

He was dry. It takes everything he's got to keep the seven-iron from following the ball into the lake. Jones begins muttering out loud, "There's nothing more maddening in the world than playing safe and still screwing up a hole. My head feels like it's going to explode."

Brockbank is pin high in regulation. Tantillo and Zydeck are each short in three, both chip to five feet, and Brockbank lags just inside them. They both miss, and Brockbank makes his putt. "Two up on the back, two down on total, and the automatic press kicks in for Tweedledum and Tweedledee. Just as I planned it, Brockbank," says Jones.

"I guess I missed that meeting," Brockbank snaps back.

The twelfth hole is halved, and thirteen and fourteen are traded. "This is getting tight," Jones says, barely above his breath as he walks over to the ball washer. "Brockbank is starting to wane. I think I pissed him off on the tenth tee. He came out firing like Ben Hogan, but it's over. After starting birdie, par, on the back, he's bogeyed the last four holes. It's now up to me, it's now Jones time. Fairways and greens. Fairways and greens. Four pars, and this is over. Four pars, and we win this thing. But wait—I don't want to get ahead of myself. One hole at a time, one shot at a time. Fairways and greens. Fairways and greens. Breathe in, and breathe out. In, out. In, out. In, out."

"What the hell are you mumbling about?" asks Brock-bank.

The fifteenth is a long, uphill par four. The chatty banter between the competitors ceased after the eleventh, and now everyone is mouth breathing. Brockbank spins out of his drive, and sends it deep into the woods along the right side. "Damn it, Brockbank," Jones barks as a Sno Ball drops from his teeth. Jones takes a swing at the grounded confection with his driver and it explodes, covering him with gooey filling and coconut.

"Screw you, Jones, that's the first one I've missed today," Brockbank retorts. "In case you forgot, the fairway is the light green grass, straight ahead of you. Not the long, shaggy stuff on the left you've been hitting your second shot from all day."

Tantillo and Zydeck snicker from their cart. Jones flashes them a frigid stare, and laces one down the middle. "Laugh at that, you sissies," Jones says to them. Tantillo and Zydeck stick their thumbs in their ears and wiggle their fingers at him.

This is fine, Jones thinks to himself, I don't want it any other way. Brockbank can pack his bag and leave for all I care. This is my match now, me versus the simpletons.

Jones reaches the green in regulation, but a long way from the hole. Zydeck hits his drive farther out of bounds than Brockbank's, so the fifteenth is between Tantillo, who sits three in the front bunker, and Jones. Tantillo is about eight feet below the green, looking at a hole cut four paces from the front edge, an impossible shot. Jones rolls his putt to a foot, walks past Brockbank, and whispers, "Best lag putt you've ever seen. We've got the back nine locked up." Zydeck concedes the putt, and the ball doesn't settle in Jones's pocket before Tantillo's sand shot finds the bottom of the cup on the fly. The hole is halved.

The sixteenth is a reachable par five, but the green is small. Brockbank smother-hooks his drive, finishing next to Jones's ball in the left-hand rough. "We can't get home from here, Brockbank," Jones says in a coaching manner. "Let's play this one smart."

Trying to stay focused, Jones starts talking to himself again. "I need to stay in the moment and not get ahead of myself. Tantillo and Zydeck—what they do doesn't concern me. I'm not going to make eagle, no one is going to make eagle. Being in the rough is a blessing because it takes away the temptation to go for it. Tantillo and Zydeck will make a mistake; I've got this hole. I'm going to lay-up, hit a wedge tight, make the putt, win the hole, win the back, win the press, and walk away with some cash. Hang on, hang on, I'm getting ahead of myself again. Stay in the present; stay focused on the now. "Brockbank, we're laying up. Let's have two shots at this with wedges."

"Jesus, you're driving me nuts with that crap," says Brockbank.

Jones calculates the yardage, figuring how far it is to ninety-eight yards, his perfect sand wedge distance. "Two forty-three from the middle, less ninety-eight, what is that, one fifty-five, no, one forty-five. OK, one forty-five to the perfect spot. Out of the rough, hard eight-iron, maybe an easy seven-iron," he continues out loud. When he's got the number down, he turns to discuss the shot with Brockbank, whom he finds already in the middle of his back swing, with what looks like a three-wood.

"Brockbank, what in the hell are you doing?" Jones screams. To Brockbank's credit, he stays with the shot. He hits the ball, though not far.

"Shut the hell up, you dickhead," Brockbank screams back.

Jones ignores him, figuring he's no longer a factor. Anyone who would hit a fairway wood from that type of gnarly lie is obviously insane. The game is two on one now. Jones creases the landing area of the fairway with an eight-iron.

Tantillo and Zydeck each have a rip at it, both missing, one to the right, one to the left. Jones's sand wedge hits about seven feet to the right of the hole, takes a skip to the left, and settles in about two and a half feet. He pumps his fist and turns to high-five Brockbank, but he's already in the cart. "Two perfect irons, and I'm all but sweeping away a birdie," says Jones.

Both Tantillo and Zydeck leave their third shot short of the green, and there are no miracles on the sixteenth. The back nine is over, 3 and 2. The press is over, 3 and 2. "If we win the next two holes, we can win the round. A comeback of biblical proportions that will be lauded for the rest of the season in the men's grill," chirps Jones as he heads for the seventeenth hole, where both teams make easy par, halving the hole.

"This is the tally so far," says Jones as he reviews his scorecard on the eighteenth tee. "Tantillo and Zydeck won the front nine, and a press, for a hundred dollars. We've won the back nine, and a press, for two hundred dollars. When we win eighteen, we'll halve the match, wipe out their hundred dollars for the total, and walk away with cash in our pockets. That's not good enough, Brockbank. I want to make them cry."

"Gentlemen, I believe I have the option to press you on the total, which I intend to do," Jones informs the competitors. "Settle down, Brockbank, you can use the money for a down payment on a personality. To make it interesting, I propose we make the press two hundred dollars, that way we've got something to play for. You two have been mailing it in since you won the front nine, and I think it's time you finally had to play with the heat turned up. Are we in agreement? Good."

The eighteenth is 435 yards, slight dogleg to the right, with a bunker protecting the corner. The green is two-tiered, and the pin is in the back right. Brockbank duplicated his smother-hook from the sixteenth hole; only this time the driving range is on the left, not heavy rough. "Fine, pick up some free balls while you're over there," Jones tells him. "You'll still get your cut of the take."

Twelve times today Jones has hit the driver, twelve times he's hooked the ball. He begins to speak to himself again. "Played correctly, this hole actually favors a hook. I can cut that corner, and draw the ball over the bunker, getting some extra roll down a slight slope. This will set me up nicely for an approach for that back right pin position. I've been fighting that hook all day, but now I'm just going to let it happen. I've got this shot."

Jones tees the ball on the left side of the tee-box, taking full advantage of the angle. Never before has he thought so clearly on the golf course. Never before has he envisioned a shot as vividly as the one he is about to hit. All the work he's done, all the time away from his family and job—it's all for this moment.

As Jones walks into her yard on the right side of the eighteenth fairway, he finds Mrs. Scaramouche already outside, in tears, and firmly ensconced in the throws of a severe panic attack. Baby Snivels is dead, and a Slazenger Balata, with a red RTJ written next to the number, is sitting no more than a foot away. Jones says nothing to Mrs. Scaramouche, but instead pulls out his cell phone and calls the pro shop to request that someone come out and give him a ruling. Fifteen minutes later, Dave Richards, the assistant pro, tells him he cannot get a free drop from the late Baby Snivels, as the ball is obviously out-of-bounds. Richards fines Jones $200 for unnecessarily holding up play on the weekend.

Monday

"Any messages?" Jones asks.

"One of the guys from Daisy Girl Deodorant is here with his son, who has a bandage around his skull. Mr. Dotage has left at least a dozen messages, and his assistant has dropped off a travelers guide to the Yukon Territory. A guy named Matt Norris is on hold, and a woman who identified herself as your estranged wife called. She and the kids will be at her mother's," Bernice responded.

"Hang up on Norris. Tell the guy from Daisy Girl Deodorant that if his kid was any kind of an outfielder he could have caught that ball behind his back. Call Dotage and tell him one of the Daisy Girl Deodorant boys is in my office and is ready to go ahead with the new campaign. Then send Lily a dozen roses; her mother's address is in my Rolodex. Gotta go," Jones instructed.

"Now, Barry, let's try to fix this driver once and for all."

Lest you forget, the purpose of this story was to highlight the defects you have as a problem golfer, and request that God remove them. Perhaps it would be best to get on your knees.

CHAPTER
7

Humbly ask Him to remove your short game.

Y ou may ask yourself, "Why would I want to remove my short game? I need my short game. Without a short game I would suck even more than I already do."

Exactly—without a short game, you're done. Everybody is done. Without a short game, Severino Ballesteros is an unheard-of manure salesman cruising for babes in a rusty pickup truck in suburban Barcelona. A bit rough, you say. We think not. When Seve, at age twenty-two, won the 1979 British Open at Royal Lytham and St. Anne's, he hit eight fairways. Not eight fairways per round. Not eight fairways in the final round. But a total of eight fairways over all four rounds of the game's oldest championship against the world's greatest players. The young man was getting up and down.

Throughout the years more major golf championships have been decided from inside fifty yards than from beyond that distance. With memorable exceptions at U.S. Opens—Jerry Pate's five-iron at the eighteenth at the Atlanta Country Club in 1976; Jack Nicklaus's one-iron that rattled off the flagstick on the seventeenth hole at Pebble Beach in the final round in 1972; and Arnold Palmer driving the green on the first hole of the final round in 1960 at Cherry Hills (Few recall that he tried to drive the green in the three previous rounds, only to miss the mark each time. Arnie recorded a par, a bogey, and a double bogey for his efforts.)—the short game has always made and defined champions.

For every hole-seeking laser from outside 150 yards, there have been dozens of chips, bunker shots, and putts that clinched titles: Tom Watson chipping in from the rough to defeat Nicklaus at that same seventeenth hole at Pebble Beach, during the final round of the 1982 U.S. Open; Bob Tway holing from a bunker on the final hole of the 1986 PGA at Inverness; Larry Mize, the following spring, rolling in a forty-five-yard chip to win the Masters in sudden death; any of a number of putts that Payne Stewart sank on his way to win the 1999 U.S. Open at Pinehurst, most notably the final putt, from at around fifteen feet; Justin Leonard's forty-foot bomb on the second-to-last hole in his match with Jose Maria Olazabal, to clinch the 1999 Ryder Cup for the United States.

Those are startling examples of the importance of the short game in big-time golf. Those who approach the game as mere pedestrians should also take heed of the necessity to be nimble around the greens, as supported by some of the world's top teaching professionals:

Dave Pelz, short-game guru, from *Dave Pelz's Short Game Bible:* "In golf, how you play inside of 100 yards is the prime determinant of how you score."

Bob Rotella, sports psychologist performance consultant, from *Golf Is Not a Game of Perfect:* "Any player, whether touring pro or weekend duffer, should spend the majority of his practice time on the short game, on shots of 120 yards and less."

Jim McLean, former PGA National Teacher of the Year and founder of the Jim McLean Golf Schools, from *Golf School:* "Since the best players in the world don't even hit 70 percent of the greens in regulation, you can see how important the short game is."

Harvey Penick, legendary golf teacher and coach, from *Harvey Penick's Little Red Book:* "As a general rule, however, the 75-shooter can become a 72-shooter only if he improves his short game—unless it was his short-game wizardry that made him a 75-shooter in the first place."

The short game. Those are the magic words.

Lest you think we've lost our way, and have suddenly begun prescribing cures for your golfing ills, let us reassure you that we have not wavered from our insistence that you quit the game. Quite the opposite, in fact. The support of the above experts is used to emphasize how important the short game is, and therefore how absolutely pathetic you will be without one. Regardless of how pitiful you currently are with a wedge or putter in your mitts, you can always get worse. Much worse.

Before the PGA Tour minor league was called the Buy.com Tour, it was called the Nike Tour. Before that is was the Hogan Tour. For those of you whose sense of golf history begins with Tiger Woods winning his second U. S. amateur title, William Benjamin "Ben" Hogan, for whom the prep tour was originally named, was a golfer of some acclaim in the 1940s and 50s. He won the Greater Greensboro Open, something called the North and South, and the Portland Invitational. Oh yes, he also won four United States Open titles, a PGA Championship, the Masters, and the British Open. Some say he had the finest swing in the history of the game.

Hogan claimed the most important shot on any hole was the first one—perhaps because he truly felt that way, or perhaps because he was very good at getting off the tee. He could also hit irons on a rope. He had to, because he was, at best, a marginal putter. His disdain for putting was so strong that he suggested, once he became a golfer of significant importance, that each putt should only count as half a stroke. Wussy.

We mention this only to inform you that one of the greatest golfers of all time had troubles with a part of his short game. We suspect your long irons and drives are not in the same league as Mr. Hogan's. So when you lose what little short game you have, it will be like sitting in the gas chamber at 11:59 P.M. and knowing that the governor is in conference with a woman who isn't his wife, and wishes not to be disturbed.

We're just not talking the yips here. Who cares if you miss a slew of two- and three-footers? Happens to everybody now and again, and it's certainly not enough to make you quit, or you'd be long gone by now. We're talking the complete and total dismantling of your game inside of a hundred yards.

The key element in scoring is getting the ball close to the hole. The closer to the hole, the shorter the putt; the shorter the putt, the better your chances of making it. Tournament flights are determined by how well you can get it close from inside one hundred yards. With your short game gone, you'll be the lone denizen of the game's first double-digit flight.

To get a better feel for why removing your short game will be an effective way to rid yourself of golf forever, we will illustrate some of what we've seen over the years. Perhaps you're aware of this old joke:

Q: "What do you hit from one hundred yards?"

A: "Three wedges."

This joke will be your life.

Chop me off a chunk of that. You more than likely do this already. We know what causes you to chunk your wedges, but it's a trade secret, and we just paid our memberships dues. Nevertheless, it's a nasty little effect, much like herpes. Always popping up at the wrong time. There you are, poised and ready to score. The target in your crosshairs, looking as vulnerable as a drunken sorority girl, and you lay a half yard of closely mown bent grass over the ball. Your playing partners, who normally are sympathetic to your golfing misdeeds, offer only barbs of sarcasm. "Throw that in the cart—I'm resodding where my pool used to be." "If you put a headstone there, you could bury the rest of your clubs." "If you feel like jumping in that hole and hiding, I'll cover you up with that blanket of sod." Get used to it.

The aborted approach. If you've ever been on an airplane when the pilot decides at the last second that he is uncomfortable with his approach angle, and aborts his landing, you can get a sense of how the flight patterns of your wedges are about to look. Let's put it this way, you can lose that divot tool. From this point on the only suspense will be whether you'll miss to the right or left side of the green. If golf had cheerleaders, your cheer would be: *Fore left, fore right, sit down, sit down, bite, bite, bite.*

To further complicate matters, if you try and stick with

the game, and attempt to straighten things out, your un-educated self-appraisal of what has gone wrong will no doubt lead you to try and correct the problem in an in-correct manner, thus compounding the severity of your misses. In addition to wagering as to which side of the green your errant approach shot will land, your playing partners will now be posting an over-under number as to how far you will be missing the putting surface. Since you're providing so much entertainment, we suggest you ask for a piece of the take.

Never say shank, it's bad luck. We've yet to bring this up, but now seems as good a time as any. You are about to shank the living daylights out of the golf ball. The interesting thing about a shank is that it is very close to being a good shot; it's just that it's not. It's the worst shot in golf. A shank is very similar to hiccups. They show up from nowhere and hang around for a while. Every person you meet has some suggestion for a cure, none of which work; then, as quickly as they appeared, they're gone.

Shanks are so bad, befuddling, and annoying that vic-tims want to lay their heads on a drill press to relieve the stress they cause. Shanks occur for a variety of reasons, none of which we care to tell you about, because you will have them for your own good. You need to get golf out of your life, and we see no better way.

Hitting a golf ball on a ninety-degree angle from the intended target will make anyone feel like a loser. Do it a dozen times in a row and we can't think of anything that should stop you from throwing yourself in front of a Ja-cobsen fairway lawn tractor. Shanks are golf's crazy rela-tives. Everybody has some, but nobody talks about them.

Yours are about to be moving in with you, forwarding their mail to your house, and taking control of the re-mote—have a nice life.

The pitch and lunge. The good news about con-stantly missing the target is that you tend to develop a really deft touch around the greens. The bad news is that your entire short game is going bye-bye, and it will be im-possible to develop a really deft touch around the greens. So there really isn't any good news. Once you chase down a pulled, pushed, or shanked wedge, you should finally be close enough to attempt to pitch the ball on the green.

In many instances this next shot would call for a pitch and run, a shot utilized by people who know what they're doing (read Tour pro) within thirty yards of the green. Performed correctly, the pitch and run will go about the same distance on the ground as it did in the air. For in-stance, if you're twenty yards away from the pin, the shot, or pitch, might go ten yards in the air, and then run the remaining ten yards to the hole. Of course, "per-formed correctly" is a term foreign to you, and since you'll have no short game, even knowing what the proper execution consists of will be meaningless.

The pitch and lunge, performed the way you will be performing it, will be the most ineffective short-game technique known to man, unless you happen to bang it into the pin, but you really can't count on that type of luck, now can you? Because the pitch and lunge is ab-solutely ineffective, it can cause scores to mount at a rapid pace. Bred from the inherent indecision and doubt that lingers in the minds of all golfers, this shot is grue-some for the perpetrator to endure, but hilarious for the rest of the foursome to watch.

Fear of failure has cost many a man success, and is the driving force behind the pitch and lunge. Once stricken with this malady, only one of two things will run through your mind as you set up over a simple pitch and run: Don't hit it short, or don't hit it long. Trying to hit it close will never enter your head. About halfway through your downswing, your brain will lock on one of the aforementioned fears. At that moment your central nervous system shifts the supervisory role of the shot from your arms to your wrists. The premise being that the wrists are much better suited for either slowing the club down or speeding the club up. That the wrists don't belong in the shot is irrelevant. Like the U.S. Army in Southeast Asia in the mid-1960s, they'll be there.

Once the wrists are engaged, your entire body will lunge slightly forward as though you are tossing dirt with a shovel. This may be efficient for yard work, but not a good move for any type of golf shot. From this point it's just a question of whether the club hits the ground or the ball first.

If it hits the ground first, some sod will be dislodged and the ball will go a foot, maybe two. If the club hits the ball first, it won't stop until it comes to rest in the rough, or in a bunker, on the opposite side of the green. Regardless of whether the ball is stubbed or sent across the green, you get to play the pitch and lunge game all over again, unless it ends up in the bunker. If it lands in the sand, we can only hope a camera crew is nearby.

The explosion shot. In Chapter Five you learned that the most difficult shot in golf is the long bunker shot. Conversely, one of the easiest shots in golf, especially for those handsome, well-groomed men with logos embroidered all over their outerwear who play golf on TV, is the greenside bunker shot. Ever since the powers that be decided that furrowing bunkers was cruel and unusual punishment for the traveling golf carnival, the short sand shot has been a piece of cake. In some cases it is a decidedly better alternative to hitting from deep rough, such as that found during U.S. Open conditions.

But we digress. For you, any shot from the sand is going to be like having a root canal without anesthesia. You say it already presents a major obstacle to shooting lower scores? Perhaps exercising your option to declare an unplayable lie every time you land in a bunker will serve you well.

The reference to explosion in this shot has nothing to do with technique, and everything to do with your temper as you try to excavate your way out of bunkers. If you remove your short game, all sand shots will feel as though you're trying to get up and down with a garden hoe. Sand will go everywhere, and the ball will go nowhere. That's not entirely true. The ball will either remain in its exact longitudinal and latitudinal settings, just deeper into the earth, or it will auger into the face of the bunker, directly below the lip.

The second result will force you to declare an unplayable lie under Rule 28. It is important to note that you have three options when declaring an unplayable lie: *a) play a ball as nearly as possible at the spot from which the original ball was last played; b) drop a ball within two club-lengths of the spot where the ball lay, but not nearer the hole; c) drop a ball behind where the ball lay, keeping that point directly between the hole and the spot on which the ball is dropped, with no limit to how far behind that point the ball may be dropped.*

Had you declared your ball unplayable upon entering the bunker, as suggested above, you'd be fine. You could take it back to the original spot and have at it again. But since you tested your luck in the bunker, and left it in the sand and under the lip, your next shot, after the penalty stroke, will also be from the bunker, because the one caveat of Rule 28 is that if *the ball is in a bunker, the player may proceed under Clause a, b, or c. If he elects to proceed under Clause b or c, a ball* must *be dropped in the bunker.* The option under Clause a is to play the ball from which it was originally played, which again leaves you in the bunker.

No matter how you look at it, you're dropping right back into the sand. This will no doubt cause a fried-egg lie. This is getting fun, isn't it?

Buried lies and, oh my, zero short game. It is at exactly this point where most everyone who has committed to this 12-step program has declared that the remaining five steps are not necessary. If this is how golf is going to be, then they can live without the game. But humor us; we wouldn't have used twelve steps if we thought only seven could do the trick. We lead busy lives, much like you, and could have used that time to work on our game, er, other projects. If you're at the stage where golf is beginning to look hideously stupid— good, you're right on track. If not, stick with us, we're about to make you a worse putter than you already are, if that's possible.

So now you've taken a drop because, well, what were your options after your ball bored half a foot into the wall of the bunker? Steadfast in your determination to get out of the bunker on your own, you will have a mighty whirl at it. This will result in either not moving the ball, or bur-

rowing into the face of the bunker. You thought the results would differ?

No short game means no short game, period. Perhaps your next attempt should be backwards. That way if
you happen to catch it flush it won't burrow under the lip.
It will scurry out of the sand and into some type grass, setting up another pitch and lunge, or if your lucky, a chip
of some kind.

Now you're starting to overheat, and who can blame
you. What are you laying? Nine or ten in the bunker. At
this point you have to be careful and avoid doing anything stupid. Not that what you've been doing in the
bunker for the last few minutes is graduate-level work, but
we're thinking more along the line of violent behavior.
You're armed with what could be described in a police report as a blunt instrument. When this feeling of extreme
anxiety rushes over you, say to yourself, "No humans. I
can't kill a human. I can justify whacking the noggin of a
small animal, but if I take out a playing partner the very
best I can hope for is manslaughter."

Puttering. At some point you're going to end up on
the green. Even if you have to yell, "Hey look, everybody, the pro's getting a nobber from the beverage babe
over there in the woods," and throw the ball on the
green while everyone turns his or her head. Once on the
putting surface, the fun really begins.

The sad truth is that nobody can putt; there are just
various degrees of awful. You're about to become awful
to the nth degree. How bad can it get? you ask. Let us
share with you a story. We know this problem golfer who
is a pitifully poor putter—we'll call him Mark. He is not
the worst putter we've ever seen, but bad enough so that

we keep him away from our children. One of the insipid games that we've played in the past while golfing is called "dots." The goal is to collect the most dots during a given round, each being worth something, such as a quarter.

Dots can be awarded for anything. Birdies, greens in regulation, sandies, barkies (wherein you make a par after hitting a tree with one of your shots on a given hole), barky birdies, barefoot-barky-birdies; eagles, one-putts, dropping putts that are longer than the flagstick; and Seves (make a par or better while never being in the fairway on a given hole). Another way to get a dot is for one of the players in the group to monkey, which is what we call a three-putt, though we have no idea why. The player who monkeys gives everyone else in the group a dot.

This brings us back to Mark. When faced with a lengthy putt from one side of the green to another, Mark, who is intensely competitive and hates to lose at anything, will intentionally knock his first putt past the hole, and off the green. Then his next shot is not a putt, but a chip. If he's able to get up and down from that point, he doesn't three-putt. Mark, however, is such a lousy putter that there are times when he will still monkey, despite his strategy to avoid such an embarrassment.

We went through that story to tell you this: When your short game is gone, Mark is going to look like Ben Crenshaw in his prime compared to you. All we can say is get used to lining up that fourth putt, and plumb bobbing that fifth one, Monkey Boy.

By eliminating your short game, we feel you will hastily come to the conclusion that golf, as a pastime, a sport, a source of entertainment, a passion, an athletic contest, an escape, or in your case, a Jones, is no longer a kick. Stunned by the realization that people have stopped giving you three-inch putts, let alone anything inside the leather, you will, if any of your neurons have escaped the numbing effects golf has had on your brain, quit the game.

CHAPTER
8

Make a list of all persons you have harmed, and become willing to make amends to them all.

It started a long time ago. We don't recall the date, but the incident is as fresh in our mind as if it happened at the beginning of this sentence. A few friends invited us to go hit some golf balls. Since that activity wasn't in the top ten list of things our parents warned us against (well-intended, but obviously misguided parents), we went along. We took a few practice swings—it seemed easy enough—and then started for real. Nothing spectacular happened, but after a few swipes we felt as though we were grasping it.

We topped a few, popped a few up, and may have even hit one or two that looked decent. Five or ten minutes went by, and we developed a rhythm. The game began to seep into our souls like a new romance. We sensed a propensity for the game, and our swings began to seem more natural, less contrived. Then we hit a few balls well. Hmmm, what's the big deal? we thought. These were the first of many false promises we'd be given on the driving range throughout our lifetime.

We noticed an older man and woman on the tees next to us and we checked out their swings. Not much for a couple of old folks who looked like they had been playing the game for some time. We figured if we swung a bit harder we could hit the ball farther than they did (our initial measurement of skill). Then it happened—we scuffed one. Then we topped one about ten yards. Then the unthinkable—we shanked one off the divider that separated us and the old couple.

For some unexplainable reason, though we had just picked up a club for the very first time in our lives less than fifteen minutes earlier, we got pissed about a bad shot. Then finally, we said it: "Fuck." Those old folks next to us, the Catholic priest and his sister the nun—they're at the top of our list.

There are lists that are long, such as Santa's. There are lists that are famous: Schindler's comes to mind. There are lists that get ignored; most to-do lists probably qualify. There are lists that are short; golf courses where you've broken par wouldn't take up much space on a mini Post-it note. But the list that you now need to compile will be the mother of all lists. The list of all of the people you've harmed in one way or another during golfing-related incidents will read like a year's worth of weekend tee-times at a municipal course.

From day one, golf, which was intended to be a source of leisure and recreation, has brought with it frustration and grief. Your reaction to golfing misfortunes is of concern—it's been anything but gentlemanly. From the profanity-laced tirades, to the scowls and insults toward playing partners, to the verbal and physical abuse of equipment, the behavior that's been displayed has been worthy of a good spanking. It's time to make amends.

You may ask, "Why apologize to these people, what good will it do?"

Because that's how the program works, and more importantly, because we said so. Remember back when you were a kid and you stuck your neighbor's cat in a bucket of water? Remember how your neighbors got all upset and came over to your house and told your dad what you did, and even though your dad thought it was hilarious and couldn't think of a better place to stick a cat, he made you go over and apologize to them? And remember how it made them feel good, and somehow making them feel better made you feel better, even though to this day you can't stand cats and have to fight the temptation to stick each and every one of them in a bucket of water? That's what making amends is all about. It's the big, let's-all-feel-good-about-ourselves part of the program, but we won't be serving tofu and wearing Birkenstocks.

The process of making amends involves two steps, a mini program within our larger program if you will. As we've illustrated above, first the problem golfer has to identify what he did, and whom he did it to, which we will cover in this chapter. Then he has to actually make amends to those people, which we will cover in the next chapter.

Chances are the problem golfer is not going to remember everyone he's harmed, and who can blame him. It's an unpleasant thought, having been unpleasant to others, especially in an environment designed for fun and frivolity. What follows are examples taken from personal experiences that may reopen deeply embedded wounds that the problem golfer has bandaged in a sheath of denial. It's time to own up to the past and begin the long process of healing. As the Allman Brothers said, and you know what they went through, "the road goes on forever."

With golf being primarily an individual sport, most people assume that the unfortunate events that take place on the golf course would only have an impact on the instigating golfer. Every action has an appropriate reaction. For every blatant, misguided happenstance that is initiated by a problem golfer, all the golfers in his group will have a corresponding negative response. The reaction is not visible for the most part. As the majority of people in the company of a golfer caught in the throes of a serious meltdown will not react in the same manner.

For instance, if a player in your group misses a six-inch putt to lose a match, and proceeds to excavate a trench from the hole to the greenside bunker, chances are good that you and others in the foursome will not join in and dig a trench of your own. Most will internalize their displeasure in the name of etiquette and decorum, even though stifling an appropriate reaction can cause a great deal of stress. If this type of stress continues, it can lead to coronary disease, which down the road can trigger a heart attack when you miss a six-inch putt to lose a match. Somewhere along the line the trench digger should apologize for killing you.

Club throwing is probably the most egregious ritual of dissatisfaction with one's golf game, and comes in a variety of disciplines. There's the flip, the toss, the embedding, the fling, the launch, and the ultimate test of strength, the jettison. At one time or another all problem golfers have perpetrated at least one of these displays of anger. Now is the time for the responsible party to recall all those in his presence when an indiscretion took place, and schedule a date to formally make amends. For those not clear on the differences between one throw and another, additional detail is provided below.

The Flip. This maneuver is often disguised as an act of indifference by an experienced problem golfer and seasoned club thrower. A flip often appears to be nothing more than an attempt by the golfer to place his club closer to his bag. Because this is a hard sell from the tee or the fairway—obviously one is headed to his bag after hitting a shot from these two spots—the flip is usually incorporated with blunders around the green. Most problem golfers have learned to bring their putter with them, so they are not headed back to the cart immediately following the lackluster chip shot.

Hot, the veteran club thrower realizes that this error is not worthy of a full-blown fling; yet he hungers to exhibit his displeasure in some form. Since he needs to change clubs anyway, the flip looks like a tool of convenience, not an act of anger. It's not exactly the release he desires, but it will suffice. Sort of a like a chain smoker running into the bathroom of a smoke-free building to get a puff or two of a cigarette. The smoker would like to inhale the entire pack, but will have to settle for just a couple of drags.

With a flick of the wrist the club is flipped toward the bag or cart, as the problem golfer simultaneously reaches for his putter. The flip will either skid a few feet along the ground, or it may catch the top or bottom and bounce a few times. The key is keeping the club within a close proximity to the golf bag, maintaining composure, and making it look as if the gaffe is no biggie.

Novices will not grasp that the problem golfer's temperature is rising, and will take the flip for nothing more than the aforementioned indifference to the shot. Experienced players will immediately know that this guy is two or three degrees from the boiling point. Without any sudden movement, they will slowly step back to the outer edges of the green just in case this guy three-putts from where he ended up. The flip, though relatively harmless, is nonetheless cause for consternation among those in the know, and therefore should be considered as something that needs to be apologized for.

The Toss. This gesture can also be made to look as though the intention was purely one of expedience, and like the flip, it usually takes place near the green after a chip shot is stubbed, bladed, whiffed, or chunked.

The main difference between the toss and the flip is that the toss gets airborne while the flip is mainly a ground shot. What separates the toss and all other club-throwing disciplines is that the toss is quite often executed with a pushing motion, sort of like a one-handed chest pass. This results in the club traveling some minor distance, but still retains the appearance of a non-flagrant foul. It could be perceived, by the uninitiated, as a time-saving technique to get the club from point A to point B.

The toss can also be delivered with an underhand motion. This looks like an exaggerated flip, but does get some air time. The problem with the underhanded toss is that it can get out of control. If too much velocity is applied, the club will go higher and farther than intended. This always results in a hard landing, with the club bouncing end-over-end, bringing unintended and unwanted attention to the toss. Once a club gets a certain height, such as over one's head, onlookers begin to conclude that the perpetrator is indeed irritated, and also a jerk.

Failing to execute a proper underhanded toss exacerbates the situation in two ways. (1) It draws attention not only to the problem golfer's inability to control his temper, but also to his pitiful shot. (2) An opportunity to really heave the club is wasted. Problem golfers who are predisposed to club throwing always want to throw the club as far as humanly possible. They also know that this type of behavior will lead to permanent banishment from the game, and leave them with nowhere to throw clubs.

Because of this, they cultivate the various club-throwing disciplines and use each in the proper manner. A toss that turns into an untethered whirligig may as well be a fling, if not more. This is why it is recommended that all club tosses be made with the pushing motion. It is easier to control, and therefore rarely gets above eye level.

Anyone who has been witness to a toss, especially one that as gotten away from the disgruntled problem golfer and turned into something more than intended, has suffered greatly and needs to have apologies directed his or her way.

The Embedding. Here we introduce club-throwing action, though the club isn't actually thrown. Embedding is undeniably an act of anger, for there is no reason whatsoever to lodge the head of a golf club six inches into the turf. While flipping and tossing of the club can be written off as nothing more than an efficient means of relieving the golfer of excess equipment, there are no time-saving advantages to impaling the earth with a golf club and then withering in embarrassment while trying to extract it like a would-be Arthur taking the sword from the stone. Additionally, the club needs to be cleaned, and that usually involves scraping mud out of the grooves, a time-consuming and labor-intensive project.

There are some upsides to the practice of club embedding. One is that people are not in any danger of getting hit with the club. The planting of a club head into the ground poses a greater risk to the plantee, as shock waves from the impact can travel up the shaft and into the arm of the problem golfer who has momentarily lost focus. The reverb can cause all sorts of damage, from strained muscles to torn tendons to broken bones. There have been reports of golfers, lost in the frustration of the moment, who go to embed a club only to find that the landing area is not fairway or rough, but cart path.

The club breaks, and perhaps an arm as well. In remote cases, in the drier regions of the world, the spark that is created when steel smacks off of concrete can lead to brush fires. So there you have the club embedder, flopping on the ground, grasping his broken wrist in agony, while the rough goes up in flames around him.

The embedding of the golf club really doesn't hurt or offend fellow problem golfers, but the person who does the embedding should apologize to those around him for being such an ass.

The Fling. The fling features a sidearm delivery, and introduces velocity and distance into the picture. It is equally effective with any club, from any playing surface, and goes a long way toward relieving the stress of the thrower.

A seasoned flinger can bring the precision and accuracy of a sharpshooter to this discipline. Under controlled circumstances it's a beautiful thing to see. An accomplished flinger can stick a seven-iron under a golf cart from thirty yards, and not damage the cart or the club in the process. A fling can be low to the ground, or can carry for good distance in the air. It is the throw of choice for those problem golfers who are apt to deposit clubs in water hazards, and it is an excellent mechanism for wrapping shafts around tree trunks.

Unfortunately, most flingers fling first and think second. The fling is a quick-release, big-muscle throw, and can easily get away from the flinger if he doesn't have a specific target in mind. That's when accidents happen.

Flinging is so dangerous because it comes with little warning. Unlike launching and jettisoning (which we address next), which require windups, the fling is an instantaneous reaction to a sudden failure. Miss a short putt, fling. Slice a drive, fling. Top a wedge, fling. Whiff, fling. Skull one out of a bunker, across a green, and into a pond—fling, fling, fling. Anyone close to the flinger can easily get picked off, the result of which can be traumatic injury, or even death.

The Launch. The launch is used for emphasis as well as dramatics. Unlike the fling, the launch is not a knee-jerk reaction, but a cold, calculated incident. Generally foreshadowed with a pause after an unusually poor shot, the launch is a height and distance throw. The first of the club-throwing techniques that incorporates an overhand maneuver, this is a maximum-relief type of response to an elongated build-up of frustration. It is the bowel movement after a week of constipation, the orgasm after a month of petting.

The launch is the glamour event of club throwing. It is the power game. It is the home run, the long pass for a touchdown, the slam-dunk of its genre. It is a statement.

A declaration that says, "I may not be able to use these idiotic clubs for the intended purpose, but I am in charge here. If I want, I can throw these bastards as far as the eye can see."

Effective launches require some type of momentum, so many golfers will take two or three steps before letting go. Launchers in a heightened state of irritation have even been seen in full sprint prior to letting the club fly. To the casual observer it looks somewhat like a javelin toss, though the club travels end over end, not on a plane as a javelin will.

The launch poses little threat to members in the group because they have time to see it develop and to move off to the sides. Unless someone happens to be underneath it when it lands, it's as harmless as blue ice falling from a jet liner, but still an event that needs to be reckoned with.

The Jettison. Best illustrated by Judge Smails in *Caddyshack* when the club he threw cleared the clubhouse and landed on an umbrella located on the patio— taking out an old woman in the process. A jettisoned club is a club the problem golfer has no interest in ever seeing again. It is a launch with purpose.

The jettison represents the complete surrender of a problem golfer. While a toss, or a fling at the most, is an efficient means to express one's displeasure with one's performance, the jettison is a cry for help. It screams, "Look at me, I'm a three-putting, pull-hooking, ball-topping, shank-slicing moron."

Truth be told, no one needs to heave a club deep into woods or far into the water to emphasize how badly things are going. But problem golfers who've reached the stage of jettisoning clubs have crossed the threshold of normal emotional response with little chance of coming back to the game.

Deep down, many problem golfers believe the jettisoned club is a sacrifice to the golfing gods. As if the gods want a used, $400 graphite driver that doesn't work. Yet at this stage of the game the problem golfer has been there, done that, with most psychological treatments, including electroshock therapy, and perhaps even a nip to the frontal lobes. All that is left is violent release through club throwing. Being mentally weak is no excuse, and just because jettisoning a club makes the problem golfer feel better, and it is a form of entertainment to the rest of the group—it's not every day you see a Big Bertha helicoptering over your head into a body of water—it still can't go without the requisite "I'm sorry" on behalf of the jettisoner.

(Point of reference for those playing with a problem golfer who jettisons a club: DO NOT RETRIEVE THIS CLUB. After he whacks you across the skull with the club you just returned, he'll likely jettison it right back to where you went and fetched it from—usually with the following idiom, "If I had wanted the friggin' club, do you think I would have thrown it forty-five yards into the woods?")

Club throwing is not a victimless crime. As you can see, the acts of senseless, uncontrolled club throwing are not just mannerisms of poor etiquette, but are very dangerous to the other golfers who serve as playing partners with the guilty parties. Club throwing, however, is not the beginning and end of poor sportsmanship. Additional issues take on a less violent tone, but are no less of a concern.

Swearing. When Tiger Woods pulled his tee-shot on the last hole of the third round of the 2000 U.S. Open, and his ball found the rocks alongside the eighteenth at

Pebble Beach, NBC cameras were there to capture a moment that featured a few words that made for uncomfortable network television on a Saturday morning. He later apologized. Here is perhaps the only way golfers can be like Tiger: cussing a blue streak, then admitting that they shouldn't have done so and apologizing.

Most unfortunate phrases of displeasure come under circumstances far less grueling, or for that matter, less important, than the U.S. Open. That doesn't diminish the fact that someone was within earshot when the problem golfer went off on a rant that could make Dennis Miller blush. Screaming, "You goober-dicked, bed-wetting, turd-eating piece of puke, I never want to see your smelly ass on my club face again," as the ball does a triple gainer into a pond, will do nothing to bring it back. Nor will it endear the problem golfer to his playing companions. If Tiger Woods can apologize to a whole nation, the problem golfer can do so to a few, formerly close friends.

Poor sportsmanship. This is the catchall of bad manners on the golf course. It includes, but is not limited to, running the tires of a golf cart over an opponent's balls (golf or otherwise); running ahead and mismarking an opponent's balls on the green, or kicking them off the green all together; taking the flagstick and impaling it in the green thirty or forty feet from the hole. (Note: This rarely works because golfers never hit close to the pin. It may even result in more birdies on that hole than what would normally occur.)

Also bad form: screaming in back swings; talking on a cell phone for reasons other than personal or national emergencies; driving a golf cart through, over, and into bunkers, greens, and ponds; organizing any sort of spontaneous, non-golfing activity while on the course, such as getting everyone on a backed-up tee to do the Hokie-Pokie; actually taking one's dick out after failing to hit past the ladies' tees.

In closing, anyone who has been in the presence of these acts must be added to the problem golfer's list, and every effort must be made to apologize to these poor, abused folks.

CHAPTER
9

***Make direct amends to such people
wherever possible, except when to do so
would injure them or others.***

One of the more important steps in the overall process of quitting golf is that of apologizing to those you've harmed during your affliction. Just as your parents made you say you were sorry when you spilled purple grape juice on the neighbor's white wall-to-wall carpeting, it's now time to express regret to, and ask forgiveness from, those people who suffered during your time as a golfer.

When we last saw Bobby Jones, our problem golfer from Chapter Six, he was on the range, the Monday after an exceedingly difficult and costly round the day before. There he was, still working, still searching for that elusive something that can transform him into the golfer he has always wanted to be. The golfer that, deep in his soul, he always believed he should be.

As we catch up to him, five years since that horrid slice prematurely ended the playful and innocent life of Baby Snivels, things haven't gone as planned for Bobby Jones. In fact, the only thing that remained constant was his inability to lower his double-digit handicap. Everything else has been lost. Even an accelerated program of instruction, practice, sports psychology, hypnosis, and a brief conversion to Buddhism, failed to produce the results he so desperately wanted. He has quit the game and is trying desperately to regain some stability in his life, but time may be running out.

MAKING AMENDS

"It's time, Jones."

"I'm not ready," he responds.

"No one is ever ready, but it's time to go. Come on, hustle up."

"I can't believe this is happening to me," says Jones.

"Believe it. It's happening to you, and it's happening now."

"I guess there isn't any way out of this, is there?" he says, half asking, half begging.

"No. Besides, the governor isn't going to grant a stay for someone stupid enough to order a hot dog, an apple, a Twinkie, and a Gatorade for his last meal. I'm sure you had your share of kicks while it lasted, but it's over, time to go."

As they walk down the hall, Jones flashes back to all of the fun he's had, but can't remove the thought of all the sadness that was caused. That's why he's walking. That's why he's going to face the ultimate course ranger. The hot dog, apple, Twinkie, and Gatorade were symbolic of his former life—the meal he ate between nines for the past twenty years. The last meal he would eat before taking that long walk down the corridor to take his turn in the chair.

So this was it. As Jones sits down, he looks into the cold, teary eyes of the people he hurt the most. They told him it would be best this way. Best for whom, he thinks, them or me? "You really don't matter at this point, do you, Bobby?" a faceless voice says, as if reading his mind.

"Call me Robert," Jones asked. "Bobby Jones was a golfer. I'm not a golfer."

"You can say that again," says a voice from behind the glare of white light. A voice that sounds eerily like Brockbank's, his old partner.

"We'll call you what we want. Now come on, Jones, out with it," his escort to the chair implores him.

"The sooner you get this over with, the sooner we can get in a quick nine." That has to be Zydeck, or maybe Tantillo. The bastards. To think at one point Jones considered them friends. But friends are few and far between at this stage of the game, and those that you do have are as worthless as a handful of broken tees.

Jones's hands grip the chair like they used to grip a putter on slippery, left-to-right putts. His mouth dry, he wonders if there's something in Gatorade that makes you thirsty right after you drink it. Fine time to finally figure that out. The guests of honor, staring him down like a threesome he won't let play through, don't want apologies—they're here for retribution. They've come to see him whither away, to slide painfully into another world, taking all the agony, dread, and despair he's caused with him. Apologies—screw apologies, these people want a piece of Jones.

"Now, Jones," the tormentor shouts as he knuckles Jones between the shoulder blades. "Out with it."

"All right, all right. You think this is easy," Jones begins. "You think recanting your entire life is as easy as three-putting from nine feet?" As his nose begins to run, lips to quiver, and eyes to water over, Jones, with all of the contriteness he can muster, speaks the words everybody in the cold, heartless room has come to hear:

I'm sorry I played so much golf.

It goes on from there—ten, maybe fifteen minutes of apologizing to his former wife and kids for spending so much time at the golf course, at the driving range, at the putting green. He apologizes for missing, or ignoring, events in their lives that were important to them: helping with homework, school assemblies, parent-teacher conferences, and the occasional birthday. Baseball, softball, soccer, basketball and hockey games were routinely bypassed, as were his in-laws' fiftieth wedding anniversary, an anniversary here and there of his own, a first communion, and on and on.

When he stops, his shirt is drenched in sweat. Jones's hands are white, atrophied around the chair arms. It takes eight minutes to pry them loose. He is shaking, out of breath, exhausted. Lily, his ex-wife, looks at him, looks at their children, gets up out of her seat, and says, "Say good-bye to your father."

Golf had ended badly for Jones, as it does for so many people, and he was determined to never relive that experience again. His final round of golf came to a close on the third hole during the second round of his club championship. He had made nine pars in the first round, but was twenty over on the other nine holes, including an 8 on the 315-yard, straightaway and hazardless par-four tenth. Sitting at 92 at the halfway point of the tournament left him all but out of it, even in the fourth flight, which he had dropped into for the first time in his life. The leader of the flight was at 82, and Jones was giving that guy a stroke. He would have to play his best round of the year, a year which Jones had entered with high expectations, only to start off slow and proceed downhill from there.

The second round began with Jones getting up and down for par after an indifferent approach. A three-putt on the second ignited his temper, but he calmed himself down in quick order, and focused on the tee-shot at number three, the most difficult on the course. The third hole had Jones's number. There are a variety of ways to play the third, none of which Jones found particularly appealing.

Water to the right, bunkers and out-of-bounds left. Most of the time he would hit a three-iron in an effort to put the ball in play. With the wind whipping up into his face, Jones resisted temptation and left the driver in the bag. He pulled out a three-wood. This was a safe play, and Jones told himself that a par here would probably give him one shot on the field. As usual his thinking was correct.

Jones had always prided himself on his ability to think around the golf course—not taking too many chances, playing the percentage shots, aiming for the middle of the green. The trouble was that Jones's execution wasn't always as sharp as his thought pattern. It drove him crazy when, in an effort to play safe, he'd hit a ball out of bounds or into a pond. He used to say that hazards, like Hell, are paved with good intentions.

He knew the biggest mistake golfers make when trying to play conservative is to guide the ball instead of hitting it. By trying to steer it into the fairway, many golfers decelerate on their downswing. Jones was no different, and when he decelerated, his shots usually went left. His tee-ball on the third that day was going left from the start. The resulting snap-hook never got more than twenty feet off the ground, and headed right for the bay window of a $750,000 Victorian-style home recently purchased by Matt Norris, the down payment coming from the attorney fees he collected from the Baby Snivels incident.

Just before it hit the window, the ball dipped and smashed into a plastic Jesus that was standing sentry in the rock garden. The impact was so severe that Jesus' head was knocked off and rolled into a pile of something that had been left behind by Punitive Damages, Norris's golden retriever. Jones took this as a bad sign.

Hitting three off the tee, Jones again hooked the ball, though not as far as the first shot, and he found the deep fairway bunker that will sometimes stop balls from bouncing out of bounds and into the rock garden. His fourth shot glanced off the bunker's lip, landing in skanky rough under an apple tree. He caught his fifth shot in the center of the ball, sending it out of the rough, over a bunker fronting the green, over the green, over a bunker behind the green, over the white stakes, and banging into a riding mower driven by the real-estate agent who'd sold the house with the presently headless Jesus to the attorney.

Jones took stroke and distance for the second time on the third hole, dropping back into the skanky rough. He carved his seventh shot into the front bunker. With his eighth he splashed out some fifteen feet past the hole. His first putt, still using a sand-iron, cruised nine feet past the cup. He ran the next effort to a foot. He then completed the hole, and a lifetime of miserable, disappointing, and unremarkable golf, by tapping in for an 11.

As he picked his ball out of the hole, he noticed that a ranger had pulled up alongside his cart. Jones flagged him down, a man he now refers to as his angel—as in Clarence the angel who appeared to Jimmy Stewart in *It's a Wonderful Life*—and asked him to drive him back to the clubhouse. Jones said good-bye to his last group of playing partners, jumped in the cart, and headed home. He praised himself for maintaining his cool.

There was a time in his life when more than one club would have been thrown, perhaps even broken, after an experience like he'd just had. He sensed a sudden calm come over him. He felt that this must be how criminals dodging justice feel after they're finally caught. Knowing they no longer have to live their lives in dread. As he approached what could have been a most humiliating situation, passing the leaders of the club championship who had gathered on the first tee to begin their matches, Jones just smiled, waved, and said, "Have a good round, gentlemen." He was at peace with himself.

Jones was a bad-news-first kind of guy, so he needed to get through the toughest apologies at the start of step nine, his journey to make amends to all whom he had harmed while selfishly pursuing a golfer's life. He was determined to personally apologize to all those people, within reason, who had felt the brunt of his irresponsible behavior as he genuflected in prayer to the false god that he had made of golf.

Jones had played golf with a lot of people over the years, many of whom he couldn't remember, so it was going to be impossible to apologize to everyone. He dropped a note to those he could recall who were present during minor incidents, such as swearing, flips, or tosses. He explained his situation and offered up the basic "I'm sorry. I hope my inexcusable actions didn't cause you any mental anguish or discomfort," crap like that.

There were a handful of situations, however, that called for his personal attention. Jones was going to have to hit the road and face these people if he was to continue making progress in his recovery.

The thing about jail cells that doesn't come through on television or in the movies is how cold they are, especially the older ones. They are small, empty rooms of concrete and steel that don't retain heat well. That Jones spent eight hours in a ten-by-six, with little more than a clogged toilet for furniture, was the by-product of a decades-old grudge held by a man with a badge.

Jones had questioned if he even needed to pay David Williams a call. After all, he really didn't do anything wrong. He didn't throw a club or a fit. He didn't curse or yell, or break a rule. It was Williams who broke the rule; Jones just happened to call him on it. According to Williams, however, Jones had caused him a great deal of consternation. At one point Jones heard that Williams was so overcome by the incident that he didn't get out of bed for months.

To this day Jones agrees that what Williams did was so minor, so insignificant, that it should not have determined the outcome of the city championship. The rules of golf being what they are—sometimes archaic, often unreasonable, and even at times downright stupid—they are still the rules. The entire premise of the game is that everyone plays by the same rules, regardless of how ludicrous they may be. The one that Williams violated was so silly that it was later changed. At the time, however, it was the letter of the law. Williams, knowingly or not, took an improper drop from a hazard.

The violation had nothing to due with club lengths, line of flight, distance to the hole, or any other infraction that might have given Williams an unfair advantage. No, what Williams did was literally drop the ball improperly. The problem was that he just dropped it. Fine and dandy, except back then one had to drop the ball over one's shoulder. Failure to do so was in violation of one of the rules of golf. A rule that was, as Williams so eloquently phrased it immediately after being informed that his winning score was being disqualified because he signed an incorrect scorecard, "pure fucking bullshit."

It was too bad that Williams was disqualified. He had won by three shots, and had he taken another penalty for not dropping his first penalty correctly, he still would of have won. It turns out that Jones was the only person who saw it. He told an official, in passing, and Williams lost the one tournament he had always dreamed of winning—a tournament that his father and his grandfather had previously won, a tournament that for all intents and purposes, he had rightfully won—except for ignorance of the rules.

It was ironic to Williams, and Williams alone, that Jones should run afoul of the law because of his ignorance of the laws. As Williams said after he had pulled Jones's car over and recognized him, "Had you known that it was against the law for a blue sedan to make a right-hand turn on a red light between the hours of two and three in the afternoon on a sunny day in May, I'm sure that you wouldn't have done it. But since you did, I have no recourse but to disqualify you from driving through my town [a town that Jones had no reason to be in other than to apologize to Williams] until this matter can be cleared up." He proceeded to tear up Jones's driver's registration card.

Jones's biggest mistake, and the reason he ended up in a cell with a backed-up toilet, was that he echoed Williams's opinion of so many years ago when he responded, "That law's pure fucking bullshit." As chief of police, Williams thought it would be in the best interest of the community if Jones cooled his heels in the courthouse lockup, circa 1937.

When Williams finally asked Jones what he was doing way out in the boonies, Jones explained his desire to apologize for the city championship incident. The chief told him that many years from now he might want to apologize for locking him up, but he doubted it.

Olivia Bounds really wanted Bobby Jones to take her to the senior prom. Jones, on the other hand, didn't care much. Girls were an afterthought to him back then, which meant that they were thought about only after he had played golf, if at all. His buddies, especially those who didn't golf, thought he was nuts. This was primarily because they all knew, or at least theorized, that Olivia was, well, accessible.

When it came to matters of male/female relations, Jones was a bogey player at best. Even at age seventeen he was clueless as to what being accessible was all about, and what, if anything, it meant to him. Olivia, however, did know what it could mean to Jones, and she also knew where to find him—at the golf course.

Three weeks before the prom Jones was practicing long bunker shots at dusk on the back nine of his home course, when he heard a golf cart come up over a hill—

it was Olivia. They traded small talk, though she did most of the talking. "How are classes going? Have you selected a college? Did you hear about so-and-so, did you hear about such-and-such? If you promise to take me to the prom, I'll give you the blow job of your life." That sort of stuff.

Jones was intrigued. This procedure had generated tons of positive buzz in the boys locker room, but was an uncharted course for him. Given his inexperience, it wasn't going to be hard for Olivia to live up to her end of the bargain. So Jones acquiesced—one can only practice long bunker shots for so long, and a guy's got to start somewhere. He jumped into Olivia's cart. It was sort of like a Springsteen song, except instead of a Chevy they had an E-Z-Go, and the Jersey shore was the drop zone next to the pond at the short, par-three sixteenth.

Three weeks later, while Olivia sat at home intermittently crying and plotting his dismemberment, Jones was at the driving range with a group of underclassmen trying to hit balls for quarters into the 100-, 150-, 175-, and 200-yard signs. It didn't occur to him that he had anywhere else to be until the floodlights went out, and they were told to go home and get a life.

Twenty years didn't look bad on Olivia. When Jones showed up at her door, she just stared in amazement. She looked much like he remembered her, except eyeliner wasn't running down her cheeks as it was when he finally showed at her parents' house, three hours late, on the night of their senior prom. She asked him what he could possibly want. Jones explained; she nodded, asked him if he would wait a moment, and turned back into the house.

Three minutes later she appeared at the side of the house, called for Jones, and gestured that he walk over to her. Thoughts of that evening on the golf course long ago snuck into his mind, but they were quickly replaced by absolute terror when she opened her backyard gate and said, "That's the asshole I've been telling you about for all these years—sic him."

On the way to the hospital the paramedic told Jones that he did the right thing by balling up on the ground and playing dead, that rottweilers do the most damage when they get a free shot at limb. The stitches were removed two weeks later, and Jones resumed the journey.

"He's the one in the corner, with the broom."

"What's he sweeping up?" Jones asked.

"Nothing. He stands there all day and sweeps back and forth. He's on his third set of tiles."

The attendant pointed to a tall man in green overalls whom twenty years ago Jones had known as Ray Sullivan. Gifted with a smooth swing and a sweet disposition, Sullivan hit long irons that sounded like bottle rockets as the ball left the clubface, worked the ball with every club in his bag, and rolled putts like they were on a Hot-Wheels track.

He was their high school's number one golfer from freshman orientation through the state championship of senior year. From his fifteenth birthday on Jones never saw him shoot above 80. He was breaking par more often than not from his sophomore year forward. He received letters and phone calls from Arnold Palmer and Jack Nicklaus, each with a particular bend as to why Wake Forest or Ohio State would be a great school to attend.

As Jones walked toward him, he noticed Sullivan's eyes. He still had those confident eyes; eyes that could chill an opponent while simultaneously reassuring a team-mate that victory was near. He stood alone, focusing on the job at hand, staring down the target as on so many birdie putts. From Jones's right, a woman, in a hurry, intercepted him.

"You shouldn't be here," the nurse said sternly, stepping in front of Jones.

"I'm here to apologize."

"The time for that has long come and gone. Now just leave," she said.

Since they had never met, Jones guessed that she knew him from pictures. He had heard that part of Sullivan's treatment was to reintroduce him to people from his past through photos. Given the look of things, she probably hadn't gotten the courage to show him Jones's photo yet, even after twenty years.

"You must leave, now," she demanded.

"Listen, I've got to do this, not just for him, but for me also. It's part of my program," Jones responded.

"I have little concern for your program. I'm sure Ray would feel the same, if he could feel at all. I see no good in you being here, so it would be best if you stopped being here," the nurse said.

As a senior Sullivan had won his third consecutive state championship. All that was left was to choose which free ride to accept. He had kidded Jones from time to time that if he wanted to he could package him, force the college he signed with to give Jones a scholarship too. But that wasn't going to work. Jones wasn't good enough to carry Sullivan's clubs, let alone play on a Division I level.

Maybe it was jealousy, or more likely immaturity, that made Jones do what he did on that first warm day in the spring of their senior year. They cut the last class of the day and headed to the golf course, clubs still in the trunk from the previous fall. Sullivan birdied the first three holes. It looked like he hadn't been without a club in his hand for more than thirty minutes all winter. As he got over his tee-shot on the fourth, a 189-yard par three with water on three sides, Jones snapped.

"You will have to leave, now!" the woman screamed. Not the best thing to yell in a group home for the mentally impaired. All of the residents stopped what they were doing and scampered for the door. Everyone except Sullivan—it was obvious he wasn't going anywhere. He just slowly lifted his head to see what the fuss was about. It was then that Sullivan and Jones's eyes met for the first time since they skipped Mrs. Master's Zen and Emerson class to play a round of golf twenty years ago.

"Ahhhhhhhhh, Fart Boy," he screamed as he spotted Jones. "Kill him. Kill the Fart Boy. Please, someone help me. I must kill the Fart Boy."

Jones was able to duck away from the first swipe of Sullivan's broom, but the gust of air it created knocked Jones's glasses off. Sullivan had always generated enormous clubhead speed. Jones wasn't so lucky on the second go-round, as Sullivan delivered an overhand blow with the skill and force of a woodsman, into Jones's right shoulder, which sent him to the ground. The nurse tried to get between them, but she caught a butt-end under the rib cage and ended up in a pile next to Jones on Sullivan's well-swept floor. Jones took three more violent blows to his neck and head before a pair of orderlies separated Sullivan from the broom.

They could have gotten in sooner, but like NHL linesmen, they let the two of them wear themselves out before jumping into the fray. Jones took the nurse's Reebok to the groin as a final parting shot before the two large attendants pried Sullivan off of him and dragged the nurse away from the heap.

Going through life being known as the Fart Boy had some drawbacks. There was many an occasion when Jones thought it would be him standing in a corner with a broom and a drool, given the intense harassment one endures as the Fart Boy. Walk into a restaurant: "Hey, Fart Boy, what'll you have with your beans?" At a movie: "Don't cut one during the make-out scenes, Fart Boy." Worst of all, as Jones walked to the podium to receive his high-school diploma, the student body chanted, "Fart Boy, Fart Boy, Fart Boy." And people had to ask why Jones went to college out of state.

Regardless of what folks said, the incident that left Sullivan in this catatonic state was not a premeditated breaking of the wind. It was not something that Jones had devised and scripted over a period of months. They lunched at Taco Bell that afternoon, and Jones had an extra order of pintos and cheese to go with his bean burrito supreme and enchurito plate. Only after it became clear to Jones that he was going to have to release an excess build-up of air from his bowels did he decide, to his life-long regret, to calculate its exit to coincide with the top of Sullivan's back swing. Not an easy thing to do, by the way. An accomplishment in precision timing that was forever overshadowed by the resulting mental collapse of Jones's former friend.

One may surmise that a golfer should not fart while another golfer begins his descent to the ball. All rules of etiquette in a gentleman's game would preclude such nonsense. It is true, however, that since there is no specific language in the rules of golf prohibiting anyone from farting at any time during a match, technically Jones did nothing wrong. Even though letting loose with an elongated poop belch, complete with requisite aroma, and hints of moisture and texture, at the peak of Sullivan's back swing was well within Jones's right, in hindsight it seemed very inappropriate.

Jones easily could have let out intermittent, minor bursts while walking down the fairway. Instead, he slowly constructed it to the point that he had become bloated with noxious gasses, the end result being a robust discharge that echoed across the golf course—his personal magnum opus of flatulence. Upon hearing Jones's expulsion of air, Sullivan jerked at the top. He caught the ball fat at impact, carved out a good foot of turf, and chipped a bone in his wrist. He was never the same.

The scholarship he received from the University of Houston was revoked when one of their star players complained that Sullivan's constant spasms made him nervous. He came home and tried out at a couple of junior colleges. Even those programs don't need golfers who can't break 90, and wake up in the middle of the night screaming "Kill the Fart Boy!"

Though making amends is a very important element in the overall program, it is to be done so without bringing harm to anyone in the process. With Jones battered and bloodied on the floor, the nurse hyperventilating alongside of him, and Sullivan being bundled into a straitjacket, Jones decided he had caused more harm than good. Sullivan was moved to the bottom of the list.

Kyle and Adrian were high-school sweethearts. They were inseparable throughout their senior year. They had many of the same classes and went to all of the dances, parties, and games together. Both of them even enjoyed golfing, and they were good enough to play on the varsity team—together. Kyle and Adrian were Jones's, and many others', first introduction to the idea that sometimes girls don't like boys, sometimes girls like girls. A concept that later in life would fascinate Jones, but initially just served to confuse. Kyle and Adrian starred on their school's conference champion women's golf team.

Their preference for each other is probably irrelevant to the story, other than the fact that they are the only couple from high school still together after all of these years. Jones's visit to their home was a two-for-one deal for him, an unwelcome intrusion for them. The members of the men's golf team had always been supportive of the women's team. Quite often they would practice and play together, and on occasions they would even caddy for each other. It was on one of those occasions, the conference finals during the final week of Jones's senior year, when the men's team caddied for the women's, that the incident in question occurred.

Going into the finals, the women's team had an outside chance of winning, so when they finished on top at the end of the two-day event Jones and his teammates weren't too surprised. They were somewhat taken back, however, when Adrian and Kyle, who had served as co-captains, tied for medalist. There hadn't been a planned celebration if the team won, let alone for dual individual champions.

Looking back, it would have been more than sufficient if the men's team had just hung around for the awards ceremony, applauded appropriately, given everyone a big hug, and gone out for a pizza. Whoever came up with the phrase *hindsight is 20/20* probably did something like streak the awards ceremony of a women's sporting event.

The one lesson Jones learned—and he stressed the fact that he did learn something from his mistake during the debriefing he had with his parents and school officials—was that spontaneous streaking leaves too many variables unanswered. If he were to streak again, he told them, he would definitely plan ahead. Not amused, they took away his golfing privileges for a month.

The men's team quickly adjourned to the clubhouse after the last hole to grab a snack and drink before the presentations. Over the ensuing years there was much finger-pointing as to who was the instigator of this charade. Initially, it was in order to lay blame. As time wore on, however, it became a source of pride. Regardless of whose idea it was, by the time the table and the trophies were set up around the eighteenth green, six teenage boys had stripped down to their socks and golf shoes, and stood good to go in the cart garage that served as their staging area.

As Adrian and Kyle were announced, and requested to accept the team championship trophy and their medals, the men's team took off from between the carts. No one was quite sure what was happening at first, other than a lot of noise. But when they came around the clubhouse, screaming like rabid banshees, spikes clicking and clacking on the cart path, dicks flapping against their thighs, and swinging head covers around with both arms, there was little doubt. The only thing missing was Wagner's *Die Walküre*.

Everyone's eyes were as big as the guy's in the fishing boat in *Caddyshack* right before he bailed to get out of the way of Al Czervic's yacht. Somehow Jones got into the lead, and went right through a greenside bunker as he headed for the awards table. Still yelling and howling, he quickly turned his head to see where the rest of his team-mates were. None had even reached the sand before they aborted the mission.

Now in the middle of the eighteenth green, and flying solo, Jones returned his head forward. In the brief second it took for him to check on his troops and look back again, Kyle and/or Adrian bobbled the exchange of the championship trophy, and it fell right into Jones's path. As his mother reminded him, in a way only a mother could at a time like this, it was a good thing he had golf shoes on or he could have broken a toe tripping over the trophy.

It's hard to judge what was the most humiliating aspect of the event. Falling while stark naked in front of fifty or so high-school girls didn't do much for his self-esteem. Having to get dressed, and then come back out to repair the knee and elbow marks he left on the green was a healthy serving of humble pie. But Jones guessed the worst of it was the landing. His body was situated in such a way that as he hit face-first into the putting surface, his penis entered the cup.

There were the obligatory comments about his size, or lack thereof. Questions were raised as to whether Jones had any long-term intentions, or if he was just another man taking advantage of a vulnerable putting green. Then Adrian stated, loudly and clearly, "That's a hell of a way to pop your cherry, Fart Boy."

Teenage girls can be so cruel.

Adrian and Kyle didn't ask Jones in, so he just told his story at the front door. They slammed it in his face before he could finish.

*   *   *

Mrs. Scaramouche, the person outside of his immediate family that Jones owed the biggest apology to, was gone. She never recovered from the emotional and psychological trauma caused by the brutal slaying of Baby Snivels at the hand of Jones's wayward tee-ball the morning of his final grudge match with Tantillo and Zydeck. She died, secluded in the library of her Tudor alongside the eighteenth hole, surrounded by hundreds of pictures of Baby Snivels, the stuffed schipperke at her side. There was, however, one last apology that needed to be made. Jones needed to go see the Daisy Girl Deodorant boys.

Jones grabbed a box of Ding Dongs and headed out. He knew this was going to be one of the hardest meetings of all, on par with facing his family. The damage he caused the Daisy Girl Deodorant boys was immense, and it would probably never be reversed.

He pulled a hat down tight on his head and threw on a pair of sunglasses as he pulled into the parking lot; the fewer people to recognize him the better. Parking his car, he got out and took the long way to his destination, avoiding any potential run-ins. He walked behind a building and through a collection of pines, up to the area where he knew, without inquiring, he would find the Daisy Girl Deodorant boys.

He paused for a moment and took in the situation. It had been a while since he had been in this environment, and his hands began to shake. This was going to be tough, but he told himself that if he could get through this, he could get through anything, and he would be well on his way to continuing his recovery.

Jones walked out of the trees and stepped onto the practice range of his old course for the first time since the morning of the club championship more than three years ago. There he found the Daisy Girl Deodorant boys, beating balls and hard at work on their games, with Barry, his former instructor, at their side. Jones had turned them into golf junkies. He could think of no greater sin to commit against another human being.

It took a moment, but the Daisy Girl Deodorant boys finally noticed him. "Hey, Jonesy, over here," one of them yelled. "How the hell are you? Man, it's been a long time. Hey, look, guys it's Jonesy." It was unbearable.

"Hey, Bobby, long time no see," called out the Daisy Girl Deodorant guy whose son was hit by Jones's shanked wedge.

"People call me Robert now," said Jones.

"Yeah, whatever. It's great to see you."

"Sorry you lost your job," said the third Daisy Girl Deodorant guy. "We really fought for you. We told Dotage that you were our man, but he wouldn't listen. He hired some loser who doesn't golf. Can you believe that? Bad move on his part, because we're here all of the time. You have to pry us out of here—right, Barry?"

"Hey, look," the second interrupted. "Barry's here working with us, and has he been a huge help. It's almost impossible to believe he couldn't get you straightened out. Hey, guess what . . ."

"Yeah, guess what, Jonesy," said the first to greet him.

"You'll never guess," the third chipped in. "In a million years you'll never guess."

This was excruciating. Like introducing someone to your wife, and then that person ends up stealing her away from you. "Well, I came here to tell you guys something, but you're so excited, why don't you tell me your news first," said Jones, who could barely stand to look at the human train wreck he had created.

"WE ALL BROKE PAR LAST WEEK," the Daisy Girl Deodorant boys said loud and proud.

A deep, cold silence came over Jones. Not unlike the silence that came over people when they saw the *Challenger* Space Shuttle explode. He stood there, numb, like he had a head full of Novocain, unable to put his thoughts into words.

"What did you want to tell us?" the Daisy Girl Deodorant guys chirped.

"I brought Ding Dongs."

CHAPTER
10

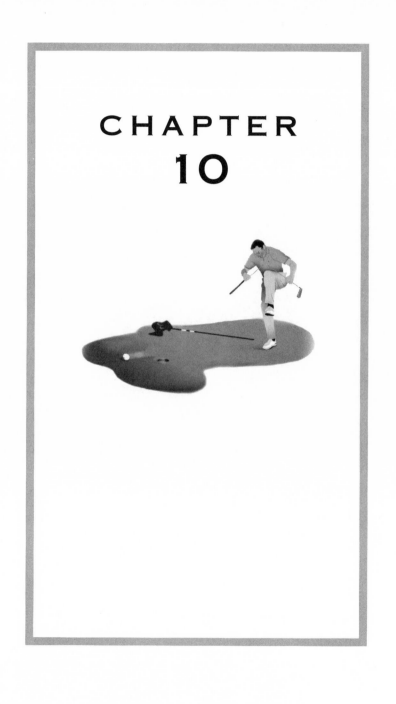

Continue to take personal inventory.

It's garage sale time. Not only will the vestiges of a life gone wrong be removed and thousands of square feet be freed up, but cold, hard cash shall be raised. Once you fire sale your inventory of useless golf paraphernalia, you should have enough working capital to engage in one of the new hobbies mentioned in Chapter Three.

Problem golfers are the pack rats of the sporting set. With ancestral links to the perpetually frugal Scots, they experience the notion of discarding anything that one day may again serve some useful purpose, no matter how remote, as cause for a queasy stomach and a poor night's sleep. Give away the putter that delivered six consecutive one-putts in a high school match twenty-five years ago— utter nonsense. It may someday crawl out from under a pile of moldy lint screens to putt again.

The problem golfer's basement, garage, attic, den, fruit cellar, cubbyhole under the stairs, guest bedroom, front hall closet, pantry, tool shed, crawl space, and trunk of his car are loaded with golf stuff. That every nook and cranny that the problem golfer can find is crammed with performance-enhancing clubs, gadgets, videos, books, training aids, magazines, faxes, and notes just feeds the fact that no matter what anyone does, no one will ever improve his golf game.

Just like a used car dealer's TV commercial, with the salesman standing on the hood of Dodge screaming, "Everything must go," everything must go. Let us now peer through a sample collection of this hoard, explaining how terribly inefficient and useless this material is.

Drivers. No one needs seventeen drivers. Stacked up like cornrows along a wall, discarded with as much ease as they were purchased, drivers stand as testament to the confounded nature of the game. They have absolutely zero utility outside of the golf course, and don't provide much more while on it.

Nowhere did golf's technology boom have more of an impact than on the driver. From the birth of the Bertha to the springlike effect of the Callaway ERC II, and everything in between, each new season has advances in metals, shapes, and sizes, forcing golfers into acquiring the latest and greatest as they rolled off the line.

The ability to drive the ball straight and long has become a prerequisite to playing the game successfully. That virtually no one can do this with any consistency, and yet the game still flourishes, attests to the madness of the sport and of those that play it. Looking for a driver that will deliver the ball a great distance from the tee, while keeping it in the fairway, is in itself a quixotic search for something slightly more elusive than a high-handicap scramble partner that can drain everything from inside twenty feet. Any sane person (read non-golfer) could have used the time spent searching for the ultimate driver to achieve monumental successes in almost any endeavor she chose. Yet the problem golfer used this time to find a few more yards, and a foot or two of direction.

These retired drivers, scattered throughout the corridors of the problem golfer's domain, ultimately come to symbolize utter failure. After everything is said and done, he is left asking himself the following question: How many different ways, and at what total cost, have I found to hit my tee-shot into the backyard of the nasty lady with the mean dog who lives on the eleventh hole of my club?

Irons. Barbecue spits, marshmallow roasting sticks, scarecrow poles, ladder rungs, fencing foils, punji sticks— all good alternative uses for used irons.

The great marketing triumph of the twentieth century was not brand imaging (i.e., Coca-Cola, Disney, McDonald's). It was not persuading suburban housewives that they needed an off-road vehicle to pick up dry cleaning. It certainly wasn't persuading Americans to retrofit their homes to give them access to more than two hundred channels of televised hooey at the touch of a remote control button.

No, the greatest marketing success of the past century was convincing golfers that if they are having trouble hitting one of their irons, for instance their three-iron, they need to get an entire matched set of new irons.

If someone blows out a tire, he doesn't get four brand-new tires. If someone breaks a dinner plate, she doesn't purchase eight new place settings. Yet, if a golfer can't hit his three-iron—and the fact that almost no one can hit a three-iron shouldn't be lost in all of this—he goes out and buys an entire set of new irons, regardless of how well he may hit any of the others.

This phenomenon results in a glut of surplus irons, many in perfectly decent working order, lying about the place. There isn't a basement of a problem golfer in America that doesn't house at least two sets of irons. It's been estimated that if we melted down all of the unwanted irons in this country, we could build a fleet of nuclear aircraft carriers.

Wedges. As we pointed out in Chapter Seven, when it comes to the short game, most golfers suck. What clubs are mostly used for the short game? Wedges. The diagnosis of most golfing ills has always been "It must be the clubs." Knowing that short-game woes must be the fault of the clubs, golfers went out and bought a new wedge. The current remedy, however, is to buy a host of new wedges.

We're not dealing with just pitching and sand wedges anymore. This is the era of specialization; golfers need a wedge for any and all potential circumstances. There are strong wedges, soft wedges, in-between wedges, lob wedges (in sixty- and sixty-four-degrees), rusty wedges, chrome wedges, black wedges, diamond-faced wedges, and even extraterrestrial wedges.

Short-game guru Dave Pelz recommends carrying four wedges. To make room in the bag he suggests removing the three-iron. His take is that the only purpose a three-iron serves is to line up the golfer's feet when he's practicing his wedges. It only stands to reason that with four wedges in the bag, if the golfer can't hit one of them, he goes out and buys four new ones.

The truth is this: Golfers should go through wedges

about as often as Catholics go through popes. There is no other part of the game that can be so dramatically improved through practice as the short game. Paraphrasing Pelz again, golfers can hit three- and four-irons all day, every day, and still not improve enough to make a measurable difference in their score. But spend that kind of time with the short game, and watch that handicap plummet.

The problem with applying Pelz's thinking to practical matters is that most problem golfers are not sweat-equity guys. The general assumption with this crowd is that all golfing errors can be solved through infusion of additional capital. The net result is an increase in personal wedge inventory with minimal decrease, if any, in overall scores.

Putters. The funny thing is, putting really isn't that difficult. You pull the putter back and pull it forward. What's the big deal? It is also the least physically demanding activity in all of sport. A third-string quarterback manning a clipboard expels more energy on a Sunday afternoon than a golfer in a year's worth of putting. Yet many a problem golfer has withered away his children's tuition money on thirty-five-inch shafts with funny-looking heads.

More putters have been abandoned than all drivers, irons, and wedges combined. There are people who long ago gave up the game but still have old putters in their homes. There are people who have never golfed that have old putters in their homes. There are people who live in huts, deep in the Amazon rain forests, and haven't the foggiest notion of what golf is, who have old putters in their homes. When life is finally encountered in far-away galaxies, these beings, whatever they are and however they live, will have old putters in their homes.

Putters are slammed, damned, and tossed aside like used swizzle sticks, accused of the ruination of the entire game with the ubiquitous phrase "if I could only putt." (Here's a hint: If you could putt, some other part of your game would be screwed up. It's this sort of insanity that should confirm that there is no other option than to quit the game). Putters are more likely to find air, be bent over a knee, wrapped around a tree, or left for dead on the side of the road than any other club. Putters, in essence, are golf's whipping boys. Taking all the blame, while receiving rare acclaim, putters are the antagonists in the ultimate love-hate relationship in all of society.

As problem golfers slide from the early stages of their disease into the abyss of being clinical, they try many things in order to use golf clubs properly. We know from empirical research and casual observation that consistently hitting a golf ball correctly is not humanly possible. Regardless of these findings, the problem golfer will spend a stock manipulator's fortune on what the trade refers to as training aids, but what we affectionately call gadgets and gizmos. These items, though created to help the golfer, only serve to push him closer to insanity.

The USGA strictly forbids the use of any of these gizmos during competition on the course. So the irony is that you may be able to develop the perfect swing by strapping one of these gadgets on, but you sure as hell can't use it where it matters and is needed most—in a match. Here's a glimpse of the type of things that can be found littered through the problem golfer's life.

Greg Norman's Secret. We saw Johnny Petraglia wearing one of these things at the Brunswick Professional

Bowlers Association Senior National Championship at Airport Lanes in Jackson, Michigan. Must work—he made it to the shoot-out round. No one is quite sure what this thing is supposed to do, though it claims it will set the stage for a satisfying golf vacation. All we do know is that since it came on the market Norman suffered a heart-breaking collapse in the final round of the Masters, virtually disappeared from PGA leader boards, and has had shoulder and hip surgery. Perhaps our parents were right when they told us not to tell secrets.

The Holocator. It's this type of thing that makes the game fun, and is probably one of the main reasons that people who seriously want to quit the game can't give it up. Straight from the company's marketing material: *Your new Holocator is designed to compute the resultant of two geometric variables. 1. The degree of slope to the ground where your ball lies. 2. The loft of the club to be used for the shot. It automatically computes the geometry of the shot, indicating the proper club alignment and direction of swing to send your ball right to the target.* We can't believe we didn't come up with this thing.

The Impact Bag. Claiming that there is only one moment of truth in the golf swing—the point of impact—this product asserts that it will teach the correct position and feel for that moment. It also provides an "auditory feedback" by producing a really loud pop when the bag is struck. This theoretically is a positive motivator for greater distance. We know golfers who have taken this concept a step further and had a picture of their ex-wife silk-screened on the bag.

The SwingLINK. This thing would make the Marquis de Sade quiver in fear. Nothing short of prime evil bondage from the David Leadbetter school. We quote from the advertisement: *You strap it on. You make your pass. Automatically, the device steps in and literally forces an athletic motion. Your body is active . . . hands and arms are passive.* Enough already, you're making us hot. Buy a couple of SwingLINKs, bolt Leadbetter's *SwingCHECK* mirror to the ceiling, order in some Thai food, grab a couple of bottles of chardonnay, take the phone off the hook, and make a weekend out of it.

The Whippy Tempo Master. You're a naughty little golfer, aren't you? Whack. Your take-away is much too fast. Whack. Your downswing is also too fast. Whack. Are you going to slow that swing down for Momma, or are you going to keep on being a bad little rope hooker? Whack. From the golf professional to the professional dominatrix, no one should be without the Whippy Tempo Master.

Plane Sight Laser. Everyone has sat through a tedious presentation where the speaker points to a screen and a little red dot shows up. Obviously the guy who came up with this golf aid managed to stay awake during one of these presentations, and devised the idea of strapping a laser on the butt-end of a club.

As the club is taken back, a red dot appears on the ground, and if this exercise is done indoors, up the side of a wall. The dot then travels back over the same path—or should, if the swing is on plane—during the downswing. The one problem we have with this is that in order to see if the swing is on plane, the golfer needs to move her head to follow the red dot. This really kills the idea of keeping an eye on the ball. The good thing about the Plane Sight Laser is that after the golfer realizes this drill makes her dizzy, she can use the device when making really boring presentations.

John Daly's Power Groove. The device that Big John used to clear the Grand Canyon. Geared to train muscles and memorize rhythm and balance, all things that Big John has a great handle on. Interesting if for no other reason than the ability to use a "Gyro" coupler, which hinges the contraption to the frame. If it doesn't improve your golf swing, you can attach your dog to it and let the mutt run around in circles while you sip a cool beverage on the back porch.

The Groove Tube. What yard is complete without the addition of this white PVC sculpture? Step inside the circle, lay the club against the plastic, and swing. As long as the club maintains contact with the Groove Tube, you've got it goin' on. Former golfers on the West Coast sit inside it to receive spiritual and holistic vibes from dead U.S. Open Champions.

The Klanger. A pair of aluminum rails used to keep your putter on line. Who cares if it works, we're just proud as peaches to tell our buddies we own the Klanger. Many of them do ask, however, if it really does turn the lights on and off when we use it. See above section on irons for practical uses after golf has been successfully removed from your life.

The Puttron. Remember Al Czervik's putter in *Cad-dyshack* (of course you do, what are we thinking), the one that signaled when he was properly aligned? This isn't too far from that idea. The Puttron *lets you know immediately when your putter is properly aligned to the target by emitting a steady "beep" or a green indicator light.* Heinously illegal to use during play, but it sounds like a lot of practice putts will drop. Making practice putts has got to be worth something.

The Pendulum Putter. Two shafts attached to one putter head. The stated concept is that practicing with this aid will eliminate the use of small arm muscles and hands during the putting stroke, thus developing a smoother, more pendulum-like swing. Best thing we can say about it is that following an afternoon filled with three-putts, the golfer can go back to his car, pull out the Pendulum Putter, and bust two shafts over the back bumper with one swing.

The Head Freezer. Takes the revolutionary position that golf is a game of hand-eye coordination. This device clips onto the visor of a golf cap, resulting in two strands of what possibly could be fishing line running in front of your eyes, with a small, red ball attached to the center of each strand. With the aid of two clubs lying parallel on the ground, the Head Freezer creates a visual reference to the where the ball is. Most people just use the actual ball to create a visual reference, but maybe that's the root of their troubles. And all along we thought a head freezer was what happened when we ate ice cream too fast.

Even the most obsessed problem golfer can't spend all of his time on the golf course or the practice range. Some of it has to be spent at home, where he undoubtedly loses track of time by reading about the game. Golf publications, dog-eared pages marking where a particular drill or piece of equipment of interest can be found, pile up in his home like divots on the tee of a short par-three.

When they're not reading magazines, problem golfers can peer though books, though the question of a sustainable attention span comes into play when we're discussing anything longer than an illustration and accompanying overview on how to hit a particular shot. Those who can focus for more than a few moments at a time without running to the basement to chip whiffle balls into a laundry basket have discovered there's much to choose from when it comes to the genre of the golf book.

Enter the word *golf* into the catalog search of the United States Library of Congress and more than 4,300 titles will register. Some of these include maps with golf courses mentioned, single pictures of golfers, computer games (maybe the best way to play golf if golf must be played), and entries that have the word *golf* associated with them, such as in the address of the publisher. So the number of actual books that have been published on the subject is somewhat less than that, perhaps closer to the number that Amazon.com lists of 3,000.

Some items, though not specifically aimed at the golfer, hold a particular voyeuristic interest, such as this reference:

General Accounting Office of the United States. Title: *Unauthorized use of military personnel and Government property at Fort Gordon, Georgia, for activities related to the Masters Golf Tournament.* Department of the Army; [Washington] 1964.

Given that the obsession with the game has grown to epidemic proportions, one suspects that a great number of these books have something to do with golf instruction. Many of these were written by, or at least credited to, some of the game's greatest players. Palmer, Nicklaus, Player, Jones, Sarazen, Trevino, Watson, Miller, Snead, Weiskopf—the list is endless—all have given us their two cents' worth. Little good it's done.

In 1973 two diametrically opposed books on the subject were published: *295 Golf Lessons by Billy Casper* and *Five Simple Steps to Perfect Golf,* by some guy named Count Yogi. Casper won fifty-one PGA Tour titles, including two U.S. Opens and a Masters. We're not sure what Count ever did, other than try to clarify the whole mess. One thing's certain, if it takes 295 lessons to figure out golf, we think we've discovered why no one is any good at the game. This is why the title of the 1935 book by Louis De Garmo is so absolutely absurd and oxymoronic: *Play Golf and Enjoy It.* Sure thing. We'll get right on that.

It's this type of nonsense that may be the motivation behind the 1933 book *The Golf House Murder,* by Herbert Adams. There's no additional information on the content, but one would suspect it could go either way, fact or fiction. Who hasn't given serious thought to piercing the chest cavity of his pro with the jagged edge of a recently snapped Golden Dynamic shaft after a particular lesson failed to produce the expected result?

Given the hoarding nature of the problem golfer, there's a chance that somewhere in this vast country of ours one person has shoved, in various parts of his house, all 4,300-plus items that the Library of Congress has cataloged—no doubt gathered accidentally, in the pursuit of perfection, unaware that he was amassing the world's largest collection of golf crap.

Understanding that the problem golfer, horizontal and taking rest at home, may not be inclined to get involved with an activity as strenuous as reading, the industry has been feverishly at work producing videos. These videos allow golfers to have visual and audio stimuli permeate their brains while they lie in a semi-catatonic state. Nothing is retained, but the thought that they are somehow improving their games while drinking beer and lying on the couch makes problem golfers glow with delight.

Tour players have done many of these videos. Curtis Strange's *How to Win and Win Again* is of interest if for no other reason than he hasn't won anything since before this video was produced. *Golf with the Super Pros* features super pros such as Nolan Henke and Andy Bean. Plus the obvious selections from Nicklaus, Palmer, Price, Watson, et al. Virtually all of these videos feature a slight variation of the same theme: *We're good at this game and you're not. Watch us do something you'll never be able to do, even though we're trying to make you believe you can. Ultimately we know that you've got a better chance of shitting strands of gold than you do of playing half as good as we do.*

The professional-instructor set has thrown their hat in the ring. Jim McLean's *The 8-Step Swing* is popular, perhaps because it's 287 steps less than Billy Casper's book. Leadbetter offers his advice on tape, as does Harvey Penick with his *Little Red Video*. There's a whole mess of them by Wally Armstrong, a guy who has become somewhat of a cult figure from the infomercial world. Jim Flick offers cures to the most common mistakes. We wonder if he touches on the number one mistake—taking up the game.

In addition to the traditional instruction methods, one can also view tapes focusing on physical improvement, such as *The Swing Reaction System—Biomechanical Golf Exercise Video,* which is probably doomed to failure for including the word *exercise* in the title, or *Fit to Break Par—G-Ball Fitness,* which we believe has no relation to G-Spot fitness, though we intend to rent it just to find out.

We are also offered the metaphysical improvement entries *Take Flight: Yoga for Better Golf* and *Tao of Golf.* Plus a video called *Mental Golf,* which received five stars from the people who offered online reviews at Amazon.com. Alas, the last time we checked it was out of print.

Then we have the off-brand golf videos. These include the Leslie Nielsen series, the neo-classic Dorf, and two eye-catchers, *Nude Golf,* and *Buck Naked Golf.* Then there's *Golf Balls,* starring Amy Lynn Baxter, who is famous for her other roles, in classics such as *Wet Water Tees, Blood Bullets Buffoons, Bikini Bistro,* and *Broadcast Bombshells.*

Since we've already concluded that there is nothing that can be done to improve anyone's game, we highly recommend any selections from this last grouping. Nothing wrong with a little guilty pleasure now and then.

As one can see, it's as easy to collect a mountain of useless golf stuff as it is to hit a slice off of a hanging lie. For the time being this junk can be set out on the curb for garbage hauling. We believe, however, that the day will come when this waste will need to be marked as hazardous material and require special handling.

CHAPTER
11

Seek through prayer and meditation to improve your conscious contact with God as you understand Him, praying only for knowledge of His will for us and the power to carry that out.

Golfers have a tendency to be very feverish communicators with God, beginning at the top with the guys on the PGA Tour. The finest players in the world are considered to be a very religious lot, and why not. They can do what no others can, play this remarkably insidious game with decided proficiency. It needs to be pointed out here, and cannot be overemphasized, that Tour professionals can play the game not because their relentless prayer has resulted in an element of divine grace being bestowed upon them.

No one can spam God with pleadings to be granted the gift of length, accuracy, and touch, and expect to wake up one Sunday morning, skip church, and go out and set the course record. Tour professionals can play the game because they are freaks of nature, and they pray every day for God to keep them in this mutated state.

Those who don't carry a one-iron they can hit off of a tight lie, namely the rest of us, have developed more of a me, me, me pattern of prayer with the Almighty. Prayers follow the line of "Please, God, let me make birdie here and win a skin," "Dear God, don't let me slice into that pond again," and "Oh God, check out that babe in the beverage cart."

The habit of praying for material goods—or in this case, material outcomes—must cease as we strive to become whole beings, on firm footing with our maker and ourselves. Entering a world of productive humanity can only be fully achieved by renouncing golf from our lives through prayer and dedication.

Most golfers will look at this quite skeptically, and who can blame them. Prayer hasn't allowed them to achieve the desired results on the golf course, so why should they believe prayer can help them get off the golf course? Great question. We get the answer right from the New Testament. In Mark 11:24, Jesus said,

> "Therefore I say unto you, What things soever ye desire, when ye pray, believe that ye receive them, and ye shall have them. Lest of course ye desire to be a good golfer. Then I shall make ye suffer the pains of a thousand tormented souls."

This should sum up all you need to know about prayer and its ability to improve your game. This also confirms what we said back in Chapter Two, that asking What Would Jesus Do isn't going to get you too far.

Instead of praying on how to improve one's game, prayer should focus on how to remove one's self from the game. The issue is not the medium—golfers are praying like cloistered nuns—but the message. No more praying to get up and down from the greenside bunker. No more begging God's forgiveness after a bout of blaspheming following a rope-hooked driver that bangs off a redwood deck and ricochets through the bay window installed in the home of a circuit-court judge. Face it—if you've gotten this far, there's no turning back. All forms of communication to The Supreme Being from this point forward will focus on removing, not improving, the game.

As a supplement to prayer, meditation can be a useful tool in our fight against golf. Knowing golfers as we do, we can assume that they all have been introduced to the concept of meditation. At an early age many would-be golfers repeatedly heard the phrase "Go to your room and think about it." At the time they probably cursed their parents under their breath as they slammed the door behind them, failing to realize that they were being shown the way to introspective enlightenment. Reflecting on the way things are, versus the way things should be, will bring golfers to this ultimate conclusion: The problems of three little putts don't amount to a hill of beans in this crazy world. (Why do you think they called him Bogey?)

Meditation has become increasingly popular among all who play the game. This is mostly due to the fact that the average round of golf begins in the morning and ends after dark. With time on their hands and bad shots on their minds, golfers sit and stare to the heavens, contemplating such deep issues as these: why does a slow swing produce greater distance than a fast swing; how is it possible to triple bogey the number eighteen handicap hole on every course I play; why is it that when I four-putt I want to run over small animals with a golf cart, yet there are never any small animals around to run over; how is it possible to stand on a range and hit forty-seven consecutive drivers dead straight and long, and then go on the course and not be able to get the ball airborne; if I have a hundred-yard approach over a pond, and I blade a wedge, barely getting the ball off the ground, and it takes one skip off the water, then hits and kills a duck, do I get to keep the duck; whatever happened to that girl from third grade who I helped with math, and I wonder if she's married yet; would death come swiftly if I punctured my temple with a tee?

All good questions, though none with any answers relevant to the matter at hand. We suggest that this downtime be spent more constructively, such as pondering the best way to walk away from the game with whatever dignity is left. Everyone would like to leave golf on his own terms, but like the aging quarterback who retires only after suffering yet another mind-altering concussion, many a problem golfer's last round will be his worst. Sitting in a cart, waiting while the four chops in the group ahead try to reach a par five in two that none of them has ever reached in regulation, is a great time to mull over the best way to bid adieu to the game.

This moves us right along to the reason we are praying and meditating—to gain the knowledge of God's will. That's all? Should be done in an hour or two, right? Not with golfers it won't.

The mind-numbing question of *What is God's will?* is not something that will be broached here. Problem golfers do not have the intellectual capacity to squat in a corner, deep in quiet contemplation of what is God's will. They have enough trouble discerning the procedural difference between red and yellow hazard stakes.

God's will is very complicated. Lots of big-picture stuff, filled with references about right and wrong, Heaven and Hell, translations from Latin and Hebrew, and concepts we quite frankly missed while playing pinch and tickle with our brothers and sisters during Sunday school. For this discussion we frankly aren't interested in the entirety of God's will. That can be left to people who went to college for such things. We're solely concerned with whether or not it is his will that we, his children, play golf.

God is not a stranger to the game of golf. Chances are good it was God himself who bequeathed the game to the Scots in the mid-fifteenth century as a way to occupy shepherds, intending to keep them away from the sheep on those lonely summer afternoons. But even if it was God who signed off on the game, the long-term results haven't worked out as planned. Shepherds will still have a go at a sheep now and again, and golf has spread like a backfire out of control round the globe.

Being the deep thinkers that we are, we've spent a great deal of time pondering this whole notion of God's will as it relates to golf. We have concluded that yes, it probably is his will that we play golf, but not for any of the reasons you would consider. We suggest that the following best represents what's going on:

> Forgive, O Lord, my little jokes on Thee
> And I'll forgive Thy great big one on me.
>
> —Robert Frost

For those who subscribe to the idea that God has a sense of humor, we offer you golf as his will, as his court jester, if you like. What could be more hilarious than sitting on high, looking down at mere mortals in their pathetic efforts to play the game? In response to the question about golf being his will, what if God snickered and said, "Yup, sure is." What if golf is God's great, big practical joke?

If this is the case, it alone clears up the whole Greg Norman phenomenon. Six up going into the back nine of the final round of the Masters, only to get smoked by Nick Faldo. Larry Mize's—this has to be the work of divine intervention—hole-out in sudden death to beat Norman in another Masters. Bob Tway's splash out of the bunker at the final hole at Inverness to snatch the 1986 PGA. Robert Gomez flying in a seven-iron from 176 yards on the final hole to grab the Bay Hill Invitational. The body of work regarding Norman alone is enough to fuel the practical joke argument. In its entirety it makes you wonder who, or what, Norman was in a previous life, and what he did to earn the ire of the Almighty.

But there's more, much more evidence to support our position. On the final hole of regulation at the 1970 British Open, Doug Sanders missed a putt so short that a stiff breeze could have knocked it in. He then lost an eighteen-hole play-off to Jack Nicklaus. The clothes Sanders wore make Jesper Parnevik's attire look like it's provided to him by Brooks Brothers. It was almost as if God was saying, "You think those pants and shoes are funny? I'll show you funny."

Speaking of shoes, the only excuse we can think of for putting kilts on golf shoes is that the innovator of such nonsense woke up one morning and said, "God has spoken to me, and he wants to see skirts on these shoes."

Arnold Palmer, who for a brief period of time was golf's mortal higher power, had a seven-shot lead on the tenth tee of the final round at the 1966 U.S. Open at Olympic. Palmer responded to playing partner Billy Casper's concern about holding off Jack Nicklaus for second place by saying, "Don't worry, Bill, you'll finish second." Palmer shot 39 on the back to Casper's 32. The next day Casper would defeat Palmer in an eighteen-hole play-off. This must have been God's way of telling Arnie that it was the Nicklaus kid's turn to be the earthbound goto guy.

Many elements of course design, such as unnecessary forced carries, bunkers we can't see out of, and most back tees, must have some ulterior motive other than establishing a risk/reward element. For instance, we can easily envision Pete Dye getting a visit from God while he was designing the TPC at Sawgrass. "Hey, Pete, you know what would be a gas? An island green. A par three, not too long, maybe one twenty-five to one thirty-five yards. Put it right over there, and I'll fool around with the wind whenever I need a laugh."

The shanks. If you don't think this is golf's version of being struck by a bolt of lightning, try to hit a shank on purpose. While we're talking about lightning, Lee Trevino said he holds a one-iron in the air during thunderstorms because even God can't hit a one-iron. Why should he? God has passed them down for us to try and hit.

We admit it—we bought Johnny Miller brand clothes at Sears when we were in high school. For the better part of two years in the mid-seventies Miller was golf. He won the 1973 U.S. Open with a 63, the lowest final round for a winner in the tournament's history. He then won eight times in 1974, and four more times in 1975. Somewhere along the line God must have said enough is enough, this has become too easy, try winning with these—and gave Miller the yips. Being a devotedly religious man, one suspects Miller may have even been in on the joke. Just to show everyone that, even though he's a practical joker with no peer, he still has a sentimental side, God allowed Miller to win the 1994 AT&T Pebble Beach National Pro-Am, yips and all.

What do these players have in common: T.C. Chen, Jeff Mitchell, Lon Hinkle, Grier Jones, Robert Wrenn, Rod Funseth, Mason Rudolph, Jack Renner, Mike Donald, and Floretino Molina? They were either tied, or held the lead out right, in a Masters or U.S. Open after the first round, but for the most part had relatively obscure golfing careers. Rod Funseth, by the way, held the lead after two rounds of the Masters in both 1977 and 1978, and didn't win. We're not totally sure if the joke was on the players or the viewers, but somebody got a kick out of this.

Golf as God's practical joke makes perfect sense, though we should give God a little slack here. Given everything he has to deal with, he deserves his diversions as much as the next guy. Ultimately, we as civilized people go through life searching for, and to the best of our abilities carrying out, God's will, not playing straight man to his practical jokes. If he pulled a fast one by implying that golf was his will, when all he was trying to do was get a cheap laugh, then we should be able to accept that, and just laugh along. "Hey, God, that was a good one. You really got me that time, God. Man, you kill me." In other words, humor the old guy, and continue to progress with the mission of ridding ourselves of golf.

Look at it from this perspective. If someone sits on a whoopee cushion, even if God placed that whoopee cushion on the chair, he surely doesn't spend the rest of his life sitting on it, then inflating it, sitting on it, and inflating it, and so on and so on. Well, we have a cousin who does, but that's not worth getting into at this time.

To reiterate our conclusion, yes, we believe that golf is God's will, but not for the reasons you think. We're sure you've been the butt of many jokes in your life, and will continue to be in the future, but golf doesn't need to be your setup man.

We understand that tossing the clubs to the curb is just as difficult for the problem golfer as sending a case of long necks down the drain can be for the alcoholic. The clubs, like the bottles, are the weapons of destruction, but they do represent some good times. Golf was played with friends and family. Business was conducted on the course, and perhaps even a round or two was memorable because of outstanding play—on a relative basis, of course.

A bunch of pars, a birdie or two, maybe even an eagle. But for every birdie there were hundreds of bogeys, double bogeys, triple bogeys, and others. As these numbers added up, so did the frustration. Frustration turned to anger, anger to rage, and rage to oh, the humanity.

Needless to say the bad times far outweighed the good. There's enough pain, anguish, suffering, and sadness in this world created by elements outside of our control. There's no reason to add more by playing a game that doesn't need to be played. Golf has had a good run, but it's time to move on. Hopefully we've presented enough evidence for the problem golfer to see the errors of his way and make an eternal commitment to banish golf from his life.

By conjuring up all of the power that God has granted him through prayer and meditation, the problem golfer will be able to pitch the clubs, rid his house of all golf-related items, and develop the inner strength to say, "No, sir, I have no interest at all in a free trip to Pebble Beach as a reward for helping the company meet our sales quotas. I'm going to a quilting bee that weekend, but thanks for asking."

Therein lies the rub.

The mental toughness and fortitude that needs to be developed in order to put the clubs away forever is the kind of deep, psychological muscle that the vast majority of golfers never acquire. It is this weakness, this gaping void of focus, which precipitates the downward spiral that eventually dumps all golfers into the hopelessness of despair. It's why shots that are easily executed on the range can't be duplicated on the course. It's why three-foot putts never see the hole. It's why cusswords are used. It's why clubs are thrown. It's why grown men cry.

The irony is that if the problem golfer harnesses the mental dexterity necessary to quit the game, to block out all external forces that would tempt him to play again, to remove every last remnant of the game from his home, turn off the TV during the majors, and block the Golf Channel on his cable service—if he can muster the strength to do all of this, and thoroughly eliminate golf without another thought, he will now possess every intellectual, physical, and spiritual tool needed to take his game to a level that would propel him to uncharted heights in the world of golf, and make golfers of all skill levels fairway-green with envy.

Golf, from beginning to end, is one cruel mother.

CHAPTER
12

Having had a spiritual awakening as the result of these steps, carry this message to all golfers and practice these principles in all your affairs.

B obby Jones, our problem golfer, having had a spiritual awakening as a result of following the prescribed steps, has come to a conclusion. Just as Luke Skywalker decided he must face Darth Vader and defeat him, Jones has concluded that, in order to justify his quest, for his purpose to have meaning, to sanctify his sacrifice, he must face golf and end it. The game, as we know it, is over.

THE END OF GOLF

Robert "Bobby" Tyre Jones, now 257 pounds shoved into a five-foot-seven frame unsuited for the load, had been sitting in a fifteen-foot aluminum rowboat on Bogey Lake for three hours. The only thing he has to show for it is a slight sunburn, an empty box of Hostess Cupcakes, and an almost dead Blue Gill that he accidentally rendered terminal while trying to get the hook out of its gullet. Every five minutes or so the fish flops on the bottom of the boat, reminding Jones each time of his carelessness. As painful as this is to watch, Jones finds the idea of putting the fish out of its misery even more so.

At least he isn't golfing. Thank God he has completely put that behind him. It's been six years, three months, and four days since Jones pulled his Slazenger Balata, with an RTJ in red next to the number, out of the cup on the third hole of the last round of his club championship, stated to his playing partners that his score for the hole was 11, and hailed a ranger down for a ride back to the clubhouse. Knowing that part of being a recovering golfer was to take one day at a time, Jones was confident in the staying power of his renouncement of golf. A renouncement that came particularly hard to Bobby Jones.

As a golfer Jones was doubly cursed. He could never reach a playing level he aspired to—few ever do—and he carried the name of one of the greatest players the game had ever seen, though he was no relation to *the* Bobby Jones. Growing up, he thought he had the coolest name in the world. Now he just thought it was a spiteful joke, and wicked curse, that his father had bestowed upon him.

Jones's father was a decent golfer. He had played golf in college, and felt as though he had many of the necessary skills needed to make it on the PGA Tour. There was just something, something totally intangible, missing. He thought by naming his son after the man who was showered with ticker-tape parades in Manhattan as a result of his golfing prowess might provide his kid with the last piece of the puzzle, giving his son an edge that no one else had, and lead him to become world famous in the game of golf.

Jones was given his first set of clubs at birth, which

was odd in that they were adult clubs. They were out-dated before he turned five. As a boy Jones was force-fed the game. His father was convinced that his son could become a Tour player with the addition of two things that he never had: (1) that undefined "something" that he believed he'd delivered with the name, and (2) an unequaled short game. For Jones's third birthday his father put a putting green in the backyard, complete with greenside bunker.

Jones spent many nights out on that green, his father's obsession quickly becoming his own. He even prevented himself from coming in for dinner until he dropped his mandatory thirty putts in a row from three feet. As Jones grew older, the practice drills became more intense. Thirty putts in a row from four feet, then five feet, then six feet. Then forty putts in a row over the same measures. Up and down out of the bunker ten times in a row, then twenty, then thirty.

By the time he was in his teens, Jones had developed a short game without peer. Unfortunately, Jones couldn't get off the tee to save his ass, and he generally found himself using his enviable skills to scramble for bogey. His weakness with a driver haunted him his entire life, and was directly responsible for the untimely death of a lap dog and the beheading of a plastic Jesus.

With such an erratic tee-ball, it didn't take Jones long to accept that he would never be a PGA Tour player, though he still pursued the game with a passion. His father, however, who had spent so much time and energy devising drills and practice routines to make his son into a great golfer, was not amused. Placing blame for his son's shortcomings squarely on the head of Jones's mother—it must be her DNA, he argued, his genes were obviously fine—his father walked out on the family in search for the perfect woman to sire a golfing prodigy. He was last seen hanging around the driving range at Arizona State University.

A major piece to Jones's post-golf rehabilitation was to help others get away from the game. He felt that in helping fellow problem golfers divorce themselves from golf, he strengthened his resolution and his recovery. He started out slowly at first: printing flyers that extolled the benefits of quitting golf, and placing them under the wipers of cars parked at local golf courses. Regardless of what decrepit, old Mr. Dotage thought, Jones still considered himself savvy when it came to advertising and marketing. Since being removed from the Daisy Girl Deodorant account, Jones had bounced around, and ended up selling advertising for a local newspaper. His flyers had attention-grabbing headlines:

Never Three Putt Again
Eliminate Slicing For Life
You've Lost Your Last Golf Ball

GUARANTEED!

He figured this approach would draw some interest, and get the golfers to read past the first couple of lines. He chuckled at his clever technique, realizing he was pandering to a golfer's deepest insecurities and weaknesses. At least he wasn't lying. Yes, he could guarantee that someone would never slice again. Just quit the game. It's as easy as that.

More often than not he would get chased away from the courses, and the bag boys would remove his flyers before the golfers ended their rounds. He had higher retention rates when he distributed his literature in the parking lots of golf stores. The volume was much lower, however, as were the percentages. He never knew if he got a golfer, or a housewife who was in the adjoining pet store buying catnip.

Jones knew his wasn't a popular message. It's not like he was selling salvation. Giving up golf wasn't going to save lives. It wasn't going to get anyone closer to God. It wasn't going to get people clean and sober. From the outside looking in, golf seemed to have very few, if any, negative consequences. But from Jones's perspective, from the inside point of view, golf was decimating people like some bastardized brain-eating neurosis, and it was spreading at a pandemic level. It had to be stopped. In his own personal crusade, Jones viewed himself as being to golf what Jonas Salk was to polio.

His quest provided little positive feedback. Those who read his missives thought they were a joke, then went from laughing with him to laughing at him when they found out he was serious. Who in the world would quit golf? they asked. Sure, everyone now and then says they are going to quit, but no one ever does. It's like cutting out fat from a diet—which Jones had been told to do, and planned to do once he stopped golf—everybody thinks about it, but few can pass when confronted with a plate of French fries or a bowl of ice cream. In this war Jones was a lone soldier. If people did quit—and deep down he believed that people were quitting due to his efforts—he never heard about it. He was never given credit, or thanked for his efforts.

But Jones had quit, and in doing so he believed he had developed a stronger character than most other men. It also freed up a lot of time, allowing him to pursue what he termed "the complete and total elimination of golf from the world's collective culture."

The fanatical nature of Jones's pursuit began to take a toll on his personal life. He had become especially irritating in his attempts to get his friends and coworkers to quit. He would show up at the office's golf league and bark through a megaphone (he found this device particularly effective in getting his point across) as his fellow ad salesmen prepared to tee-off.

"You there, heathens and infidels, lay down your armaments of self-destruction. Come join me on the path to serenity and righteousness. With me you will grow, prosper, and find enlightenment. Without me you will slice, hook, three-putt, and die. Come with me now, be my disciples. We will live an enriched, golf-less life, and spread the gospel of freedom from golf across the world."

As obnoxious and rude as he was to the people he worked with, at least they didn't have to live with him. He was downright overbearing and relentless in his efforts to get his children to quit. So much in fact that a judge removed his joint custody rights until he was able to prove his obsession with ending the game had also ended.

Subtlety is never a forte of zealots, and Jones took a scorched earth approach with everyone, including Lily, his former wife. His crowning glory, or the last straw, depending on one's perspective, was when he emptied her closets of all golf wear, gathered up her clothes, along with her clubs, shoes, balls, tees, gloves, bag, umbrella, and shot counter, piled it all on the eighteenth green of his former club, doused it in gas, and set fire to it.

Lily left him after seventeen years of marriage. She was a borderline problem golfer in her own right, and

Jones determined that a marriage based on co-dependency was no kind of marriage for him. She claimed irreconcilable differences in the divorce filings. This statement, as tired a reason as there is for anyone to give up on marriage, had merit in this case. She grew up with the game under similar circumstances as her husband, with one major exception—her father wasn't a domineering lunatic trying to grasp some unfound glory through his child.

Lily's father introduced her to golf, and then let her find her own level of enjoyment with the game. She slowly developed into a respectable player, participating in junior leagues, playing on her high-school team, and lettering as a walk-on in college. Lily loved the game, and it became clear that she loved golf more than she loved Jones.

When the divorce was final, Jones turned all of his energy toward being a one-man wrecking crew of golf. Where other men—lesser men, Jones thought—might have given up the fight once the collapse of their marriage was evident, it just bolstered Jones's resolve that a golfer's life was not a life worth living. All others be damned.

He was bound and determined to fulfill his father's dreams and make a major impact in the world of golf, albeit not in a manner that would serve his father's interests. He also quit his job. No sense in diddling around with something as insignificant to the world as advertising sales when the destruction of golf was at hand. Besides, everyone he worked with was too far gone to be saved. Even redeemers have to know when to cut bait.

By this time Jones had few friends left. The kid behind the counter at Kinko's where he made copies of his flyers was cordial to him. The only others were the two guys in the apartment next to him, with all the bright lights in their closets, who were constantly coming over to borrow Hostess snack cakes. To these guys, and others who had even the slightest contact with him, Jones started to be known as the Unagolfer.

Regardless of what everyone said, deep down Jones knew golf was bad for him, and bad for others as well. Look what it did to Arnold Palmer. The guy got so whacked out of shape that back in 1976 he decided that his time could be better spent trying to set a speed record for flying around the world. Palmer didn't win on the regular PGA Tour once he took that plane ride. Byron Nelson hung it up at the peak of his career to work his ranch, and even Jones's namesake, Bobby Jones, walked away from the game to practice law. Who in their right mind gives up anything to be a lawyer? Three of the most famous golfers in the history of the game just drop everything and go off to do something else. How clear does the sign need to be? Jones thought.

There were a variety of ways to approach his personal charge. One was at the grassroots level, to continue his current approach. Going from golf course to golf course, equipped with megaphone and flyers, attempting to convince the masses to quit the game one golfer at a time. There were a couple of problems with this strategy. Obviously there are no economies of scale with this type of initiative. Jones could only be one place at a time. If he was to be even marginally successful at getting millions of people to quit, then he felt he must leverage his time.

There is also a high degree of danger and risk of personal injury with this tactic. Golfers, especially golfers who don't know you, get downright nasty when you start bellowing things at them through a blowhorn when they're at the top of their back swing. He could count at least a dozen times when guys stopped in mid-swing, turned, and fired their ball at him. Two just barely missed. He started to wonder if those guys took stroke and distance before their next shot, but stopped when it occurred to him that this was the type of thing a golfer would be concerned about, and he was no longer a golfer.

Another approach would be to tap into the mass market. Infomercials seem to be used to sell just about everything, why not deliverance from golf? He could talk about how quitting golf had made a tremendous, positive impact on his mental well-being. Perhaps he could get one of his converts, if he had any, to join him on the show. He could testify as to how quitting golf had changed his life for the better. The infomercial really intrigued Jones, but the start-up costs would be prohibitive, and he needed to watch his funds. Going through a divorce and leaving the workforce can have a negative impact on one's finances.

Naturally he would get a website—*www.howtoquitgolf.com* sounded good. He'd arrange some links; perhaps even sell some merchandise such as those little paper-block calendars that have funny sayings on them that you rip off each day. This could serve the dual purpose of raising awareness and money simultaneously. Realistically, though, the Internet would probably only serve as a secondary aspect of his overall strategy. He would have to be out in front of this effort. A name and a face needed to be associated with quitting golf. Kind of like Richard Simmons and weight loss, Ralph Nader and consumer activism, Pat Buchanan and extreme right-wing politics, or Tiger Woods and golf.

Boy, wouldn't that be something if he could get Tiger to support his effort? he thought. Jones put his advertising hat back on for a minute and started to fantasize. What if he got Tiger to do a commercial, just like the Nike commercial where he bounces a golf ball on the face of his wedge. But instead of turning around and hitting the ball, Tiger would miss, and the ball would fall to the ground. Then Tiger would bust the club across his knee and declare, "That's it. I'm quitting this stupid game, just like my friend Robert 'Don't Call Me Bobby' Jones did."

Then Jones would walk into the picture, and Tiger would put his arm around Jones's shoulder and say, "I'm with you, pal, let's go fishing, or bowling, or gardening for that matter. Let's do anything but golf." Then the two of them would turn and walk away from the camera. Jones chuckled as he pictured how that would look on television. Then he stopped chuckling and thought about what he had just thought about.

What better way to stop a movement than take out its leader? If Tiger could see fit to quit golfing, wouldn't it just make sense that everyone else would too? If the best player in the world, the one human being who has the capacity to beat the game, decides it's not worth it, surely all others would follow. Golf would be over, done, finito. Jones quickly decided that this was the tack he was going to take. The only way to stop golf in its tracks was to take it down at the top. He must get Tiger Woods to quit the game, but how?

Getting to Tiger was going to be difficult. Tiger's people must have people that have people that Jones would have to go through just to get five minutes with him. The formal approach was out; he could never get through the necessary layers in order to set up an appropriate meeting. He had enough trouble just getting the owner of a candle shop to meet with him to buy an ad. Besides, somewhere along the pipeline some lackey could throw up a flag branding Jones as a crackpot, and that would be the end of that. There's always someone out there willing to snuff out a dream.

Jones would have to figure out another way to meet Tiger—manufacture some serendipity, make it look like a chance meeting. "Oh, hi there, Tiger, you don't mind if I call you Tiger, do you? I didn't know you did your laundry here too, small world. Tide or Era? Me too. How about fabric softener? Same here. Let me ask you this, do you find those Nike shirts shrink when dried at high temperatures? Yeah, me too. Man, it's unbelievable how much we have in common. Say, how about quitting golf?"

As good as this sounded in theory, Jones was realistic. Even if he could find out where Tiger did his laundry, getting him to quit would be another story. He imagined how much free stuff Tiger must get. It's worth sticking around just for that. Other options would have to be examined.

Maybe he could have Tiger taken out, sleep with the fishes, that sort of thing. Jones wondered briefly what a hit cost these days, but quickly came to his senses. Foul play was not the answer. First of all, he was incapable of violence against anything—it wasn't like he'd intentionally knocked off Baby Snivels. Secondly, the point was not to eliminate the person, but eliminate golf from the person. This should be able to be achieved without bodily harm.

Something had to be done that caused Tiger to quit golf forever, but did so without injuring Tiger in the process. He would have to do something so dramatic that Tiger would, at the moment this took place, throw down his clubs and walk away. Hopefully taking his entire flock with him. It would have to be something that would break down Tiger's psyche, precluding him from ever venturing on a golf course again.

Jones was going to have to up the intensity for this venture. This called for something more creative than flyers under Tiger's wiper blades. He also suspected that he would have trouble sneaking a megaphone into a tournament. Even if he did, Tiger had to be mentally stronger than the nitwits Jones worked with. Jones also took into consideration that if Tiger got pissed and took aim at him, there was a good chance that he wouldn't miss.

He couldn't have that. If Tiger did hit him on purpose, he'd have to go to jail—assault with a deadly weapon, that sort of thing. That's the last thing Jones needed— Tiger as political prisoner. Look what it did for Nelson Mandela. No, he needed Tiger out and about, golf-free of his own choice, not martyred. Jones felt that if anyone would be the martyr it would be him. He'd done all of the work; he should get all of the glory.

What if Tiger did hit him, but not on purpose? What if it was an accident? What if Tiger seriously injured Jones while he was a spectator? Maybe that could be enough to get him to quit. Jones would have to go to a bunch of tournaments and put himself in a position to get hit by one of Tiger's shots. Of course, he would have to be close enough so it would do some damage.

Jones paused. All of these ideas rushing through his head made him hungry, so a box of Hostess Sno Balls was assaulted. The addition of food slowed his brain down enough for bits of logic to seep in. Going from tournament to tournament trying to get hit by a Tiger Woods tee-ball was ridiculous. How often does the guy toe a driver into the crowd? The only place to get hit by a Tiger Woods tee-ball is 280 yards off the tee, in the middle of the fairway. By then most of the velocity would have worn off. Running around trying to give the tee-ball a header would only lead to mockery, not martyrdom.

What he required was immediate impact, right off the clubface. It didn't take a Jesus head rolling into a pile of poop for Jones to see what he had to do this time. He would have to throw himself in front of a Tiger Woods tee-ball. If he was going to get hit by golf balls anyway, he may as well get hit by just one and be done with it. Nobody, especially a player who creates as much velocity off of the driver as Tiger, would be able to rebound from hitting someone with a golf ball at close range.

The sight of Jones squirming in agony there on the tee would definitely be enough to get the world's best golfer to quit. Jones fully expected that he would sustain some injuries from this, but the pain would be worth the gain. He would take the bullet for millions upon millions of lost souls. All trekking aimlessly around golf courses looking for something they'll never find. He would become a hero to each and every one of them.

There is no way to train for this. Jones did think about buying a couple of cases of snack cakes, generic brand of course, and getting the stoners from the apartment next to him to hit whiffle balls while he jumped in front of them. But you don't practice suicide missions, and in the back of his mind Jones realized that this could turn out to be just that. Since he had given up everything else—his marriage, his kids, his career, and in many aspects, his self-esteem—not to mention golf, he was prepared to give his life for the one thing he now truly believed in.

To add impact and importance to the message, Jones chose to pull this off on one of golf's grandest stages, the Masters tournament. The most popular cliché associated with the tournament is that the Masters doesn't start until the back nine on Sunday. Jones was going to end golf on the back nine of the Masters on Sunday.

Logistically speaking, pulling this off would put him in a class with the Great Train Robbery of 1963 in Great Britain, the Lufthansa caper at JFK, the gold heist at Heathrow, and the Brinks job of Boston in the 1950s. Jones paused—these were all criminal activities; what he was doing wasn't illegal. At least he didn't think so. Besides, those robberies were the acts of selfish delinquents, designed to profit but a few. What Jones was going to do would benefit millions of people around the world. Whatever hesitation he may have felt vanished quickly.

On the south side of Augusta National, the thirteenth tee abuts the neighboring Augusta Country Club. There are no spectators in this area, and therefore security is concentrated elsewhere during the tournament. Even though the outside perimeter of the course is as fortified as the U.S. naval base at Guantanamo Bay, Cuba, when the last players come through on Sunday afternoon, even the most ardent rent-a-cop will shift his attention to catch a glimpse of the action. This was when Jones would make his move.

All eyes were on Tiger Woods that Sunday as he hit his tee-shot on the par-three twelfth hole, including those charged with maintaining the integrity of the fence line. While the ball was in the air, Jones struggled to the top of the fence, flopped his girth over the chain links, and bounced into the pines and dogwoods that surrounded the tee, crushing the supply of Hostess apple pies he had wedged into his jeans. Heart racing and hand mopping his brow, he caught himself watching with anticipation as Tiger made his way to the twelfth green and lined up his putt. This lapse disappointed him, but didn't discourage him from the job at hand. He turned his head and didn't watch as Tiger dropped a rare Sunday birdie at the twelfth.

Even though the thirteenth tee is nestled in a corner of the course, a good 170 yards from the grandstands behind the twelfth tee, the roar of the crowd as Tiger's group moved from twelve to thirteen muffled any sounds Jones made as he situated himself on the left-hand side of the teeing area. Jones, who was taught by his father to visualize a shot before he took it, had planned on visualizing that he was trying to block a field goal. He would break through the tree line and throw himself in front of the tee-ball.

Unfortunately, the fall that splattered his emergency Hostess rations had also done some damage to Jones's right knee. The image of blocking a field goal was quickly shifted to that of Alec Guinness making his way to the dynamite plunger in *Bridge on the River Kwai*. Either way, Jones thought, finally something his father taught him was going to come in handy.

At 5:38, on the back nine, Sunday afternoon at the Masters, Jones lunged out of the fabulously blooming flowers and threw himself in front of Tiger Woods's drive on the par-five, thirteenth hole, looking quite similar to a sea lion throwing itself off a rock and into the surf. Tiger, who in the past had been able to stop his swing in an instant if he heard a ball marker drop on a putting green half a course away, never even blinked, and unleashed a swing that, paraphrasing the late Henry Longhurst, possessed a majestic violence.

The ball entered Jones through his plentiful belly and exited out his back, taking with it a variety of organs, vital and otherwise, blood, glop, and bone fragments. The ball, covered in partially digested snack food, came to rest in the fairway about a hundred yards from the tee. Everything else littered the turf between the tee and the ball. It was a good thing this was the final group.

Drenched in sweat, blood, azaleas, and irony, Robert Tyre Jones lay mortally wounded on the meticulously manicured grounds of the Augusta National Golf Club. As Tiger Woods, seemingly oblivious to what had happened, stepped over him, Jones looked up and said, "You caught all of that one." When Tiger got to his ball he asked for a ruling as to whether he could clean it off. The official said no.

Jones was buried three days later, in an unmarked grave, about the distance of a sliced driver from Mrs. Gladys Scaramouche. Tiger went on to birdie the thirteenth that Sunday, en route to another runaway Masters victory.

The cause was noble, and the cause was just, but as with virtually everything else Jones tried to do in golf, the execution was highly flawed. There are recovering golfers who look at Robert Tyre Jones as a martyr in the truest sense of the word, willing to give his life in exchange for something he held in strong belief.

The majority just laugh, and ask, "What was he thinking? It's only golf."

You Had a Problem

As we said in the beginning, this wasn't going to be easy. You quickly found this to be true when you answered yes to fourteen of the fifteen telltale signs of a problem golfer. At first you went into denial. "These questions are stupid," you said. "Who makes up these questions? Probably some chop with a forty-eight handicap. Well, maybe he can't handle golf, but I sure can."

So you tried to prove your affirmative answers to the fifteen questions meant nothing. You could stop anytime you wanted to. To prove it you took your clubs out of the trunk and put them in the basement. You watched figure skating on Saturday and Sunday afternoon. You canceled your subscription to *Golf Magazine* and *Golf Digest*. "There," you said. "I don't need golf. I can quit golf whenever I want. I don't have a problem."

But then it started to happen. You made up reasons to go down the basement. "I think I'll check the furnace filter, honey." You wouldn't know a furnace filter if it chauffeured your golf cart. You purchased a picture-in-picture television so you could watch triple bogeys and triple axels at the same time. You were caught at the magazine rack of the local convenience store paging through *Maximum Golf*.

Then one day you snapped. You ran out of work, telling your boss that your child's head had just caught fire during a science experiment and you had to go the hospital. But there was no fire, there was no head, there was no science experiment, there was no hospital. There was only a golf course, a set of rented clubs, and a golf ball you stole from a coworker's desk that was in a hole-in-one trophy.

Everyone needs to find bottom, and that's when you found yours. Golf, just like that first love who broke your heart, came over you without warning, made you feel real giddy, made promises it wasn't ever going to keep, knocked the wind out of you, and left without asking if you could still be friends.

It was then you realized we were right. Sure, you had a problem, and golf was it, but weaker men have defeated stronger adversaries. You accepted and dedicated yourself to the twelve steps of *How to Quit Golf*. In essence you said, "It's my life, damn it, and I want it back."

Just imagine the calm serenity that will come over you when you hear stories of golfing woe. The perils and pitfalls of golf will no longer be of concern. Your house, your home, your entire self will be completely and exhaustively vanquished of all that is golf. That which for years has been your foe, your menace, your silent killer, will be defeated and dead. You, and you alone, are king of your castle.

Comfortable with your decision, and perfectly at home with the understanding that golf is nothing more than a stupid game played by dumb people, you can honestly tell yourself that for the first time in your life you've beaten golf. You have won.

You feel an enormous sense of accomplishment. Being a reformed golfer is beginning to engulf you. You have a skip in your walk, a glint in your eye. An effervescent tingle is surging through your body, and for once and for all you are finally happy. You want to scream out, "Free of golf, free of golf. Thank God almighty, I'm free of golf."

But you don't scream out. You don't scream out because all is not right. You go through a mental checklist of the process and procedure that led you to this very point: the reluctant acceptance of the problem, the pursuit of non-golfing avocations, the moral inventory, the removal of defective characteristics, making amends, acknowledging that golf is God's practical joke, and finally, trying to get others to quit.

Then, and only then, it hits you. You don't scream out because the only thing crazier than playing golf is quitting golf.

Slowly anger builds. You feel you've been duped. Led down a path. Sold a bill of goods. Why would anyone in their right mind quit golf you ask (forgetting for a moment that no one who plays golf can truly be considered as having a right mind)? Quitting golf isn't the answer to anything. Quitting golf solves nothing. This has been a momentous waste of time. Had you been practicing golf during the time spent trying to quit golf, my God, you'd be great by now.

Yeah, right.

OK, so maybe quitting isn't the answer, but what you've been doing since you took your first swipe at a ball doesn't hold much promise either.

The fact is, you needed this. You needed to have all you hold dear trotted out in front of you and slapped around. You needed to watch as we gave golf and golfers alike a cavity search for the truth. This exercise in intro-spection and self-evaluation couldn't have come at a bet-ter time. This cleansing, and the king-sized dose of humility that came with it, will do wonders for you in all aspects of your life. It has for ours.

Maybe you're right; quitting golf isn't going to solve anything, but neither is playing golf. It's just a game for crying out loud. So go on. Go and get yourself a tee-time. And do us all a favor, quit taking it so seriously, you're driving the rest of us nuts.

Acknowledgments

An enormous amount of thanks and gratitude must go to the following people: Tom Brockbank, who read every un-rewritten sentence; Jeff Daniels, who kept saying, "It's funny, quit worrying about it, and keep writing"; and Loren Estleman, whose forty-plus novels gave weight to his praise and credence to his encouragement.

Credit and applause must also be given to my wife Beverly, who wondered, but never questioned, what it was I was doing on the computer; my agent, Jim "Give Me Two Weeks" Levine, of James Levine Communications, Inc., for bringing the bidders to the table and helping me turn pro; my editor, Brian Tart; Amy Hughes and the people at Dutton, especially the salespeople who probably never get thanked, for understanding and appreciating the damage that golf was having on this country and having the courage to do something about it; Dave Richards and Kevin Frish, who can properly position anything golf-related; Ed Wendover, who a long time ago let me write for his paper; Larry Donald, God rest his soul, whose motto of "we print everything that fits" allowed me to drone on endlessly about golf; and the Tanbacks and all others who have had to put up with my nonsense on the golf course for these many years.

Last, to my mom, Janet Hundley, for no other reason than that she's my mom, and she'll get a big kick out of showing her name to everyone she knows, and even those she doesn't.

ABOUT THE AUTHOR

Craig Brass lives in Plymouth, Michigan, with his wife, Beverly, and daughter, Cameron. By day he is a financial consultant for corporate retirement plans. By night he's a golf writer, which is difficult because it's hard to golf and write in the dark. He is a recipient of the 2001 Outstanding Achievement Award given by the International Network of Golf for his columns. He has an undergraduate degree in business administration from Bowling Green State University, and a master of art in advertising from Michigan State University.